ASP.NET Web API

Build RESTful web applications and services on the .NET framework

Master ASP.NET Web API using .NET Framework 4.5 and Visual Studio 2013

Joydip Kanjilal

[PACKT] PUBLISHING
enterprise
professional expertise distilled

BIRMINGHAM - MUMBAI

ASP.NET Web API

Build RESTful web applications and services on the .NET framework

First published: December 2013

Production Reference: 1121213

Published by Packt Publishing Ltd.
Livery Place
35 Livery Street
Birmingham B3 2PB, UK.

ISBN 978-1-84968-974-8

www.packtpub.com

Cover Image by Artie Ng (artherng@yahoo.com.au)

Credits

Author
Joydip Kanjilal

Reviewers
Santhosh Aravalli
Chandana N. Athauda
Anand Narayanaswamy
Pavel Volgarev

Acquisition Editor
Kartikey Pandey
Pramila Balan
Nikhil Chinnari

Lead Technical Editor
Anila Vincent

Technical Editors
Mrunmayee Patil
Faisal Siddiqui
Sonali S. Vernekar

Project Coordinator
Kranti Berde

Copy Editor
Roshni Banerjee
Sarang Chari
Mradula Hegde
Dipti Kapadia
Kirti Pai
Lavina Pereira

Proofreader
Clyde Jenkins

Indexer
Tejal Soni

Graphics
Ronak Dhruv
Abhinash Sahu

Production Coordinator
Nilesh R. Mohite

Cover Work
Nilesh R. Mohite

About the Author

Joydip Kanjilal is a Microsoft Most Valuable Professional in ASP.NET, a speaker, and the author of several books and articles. He has over 16 years of experience in the IT industry, with more than 10 years using Microsoft .NET and its related technologies. He was selected as the MSDN Featured Developer of the Fortnight a number of times and also as the Community Credit Winner by `www.community-credit.com` several times. He has authored the following books:

- *Visual Studio Six in One* (Wrox Publishers)
- *ASP.NET 4.0 Programming* (Mc-Graw Hill Publishing)
- *Entity Framework Tutorial* (Packt Publishing)
- *Pro Sync Framework* (APRESS)
- *Sams Teach Yourself ASP.NET Ajax in 24 Hours* (Sams Publishing)
- *ASP.NET Data Presentation Controls Essentials* (Packt Publishing)

He has also authored more than 250 articles for some of the most reputable sites, such as `www.msdn.microsoft.com`, `www.code-magazine.com`, `www.asptoday.com`, `www.devx.com`, `www.ddj.com`, `www.aspalliance.com`, `www.aspnetpro.com`, `www.sql-server-performance.com`, and `www.sswug.com`. A lot of these articles have been selected at `www.asp.net` – Microsoft's official website on ASP.NET.

He has years of experience in designing and architecting solutions for various domains. His technical strengths include C, C++, VC++, Java, C#, Microsoft .NET, Ajax, WCF, REST, SOA, Design Patterns, SQL Server, Operating Systems, and Computer Architecture.

For more details, please refer to the following links:

- **Blog**: `http://aspadvice.com/blogs/joydip`
- **Website**: `www.joydipkanjilal.com`
- **Twitter**: `https://twitter.com/joydipkanjilal`
- **Facebook**: `https://www.facebook.com/joydipkanjilal`
- **LinkedIn**: `http://in.linkedin.com/in/joydipkanjilal`

I am thankful to the entire team at Packt Publishing for providing me the opportunity to author this book. I am also thankful to my wife, Sabita Kanjilal, for her encouragement throughout this project, as well as Shaik Tajuddin, Prithwish Ganguli, and my other family members for their continued support.

About the Reviewers

Santhosh Aravalli has over 10 years of programming experience in working with Microsoft technologies. In his professional career, he has developed solutions ranging from enterprise web applications to SOA applications, primarily using the Microsoft.NET platform. He has worked across many industry domains, including financial, mortgage, retail, and logistics companies in Chicago and the Los Angeles metro area. He has numerous industry certifications, including MCAD, MCTS, and MCPD and is on his way to get his MCSD shortly. He graduated from the Kakatiya University in India with a degree in Computer Science & Engineering.

In his spare time, he practices meditation, collects aphorisms, visits the library, watches TED Talks, and works on his pet projects.

Visit his blog at `http://visualstudio99.blogspot.com` or contact him at `saravalli9@gmail.com`.

Chandana N. Athauda is currently employed at Brunei Accenture Group (BAG) Networks, Brunei. He serves as a Technical Consultant and focuses on adopting new technologies toward solid solutions. He has been working professionally in the IT industry for more than 12 years (he's also an ex-Microsoft Most Valuable Professional (MVP) and Microsoft Ranger for TFS). His roles in the IT industry have spanned the entire spectrum from programming to technical consulting. Technology has always been a passion for him. In his spare time, Chandana enjoys watching association football.

If you would like to talk to Chandana about this book, feel free to write to him at `info@inzeek.net` or tweet him at `@inzeek`.

I dedicate this book to my son, Binuk, and also in memory of my father, Samson.

Anand Narayanaswamy, an ASPInsider, works as a freelance writer based in Trivandrum, Kerala, India. He was a Microsoft Most Valuable Professional (MVP) from 2002 to 2011 and has worked as the Chief Technical Editor for `www.ASPAlliance.com` for a period of five years.

Anand has worked as a technical editor for several popular publishers, such as Sams, Addison-Wesley Professional, Wrox, Deitel, Packt Publishing, and Manning. His technical editing skills have helped the authors of *Sams Teach Yourself the C# Language in 21 Days*, *Core C# and .NET*, *Professional ADO.NET 2*, *ASP.NET 2.0 Web Parts in Action*, and *Internet and World Wide Web* (*Fourth Edition*) to fine-tune the content.

He has also contributed articles for Microsoft's Knowledge Base, `www.c-sharpcorner.com`, `www.developer.com`, and `wwwcodeguru.com`, and has delivered podcast shows.

Anand runs his own blog at Learnxpress (`www.learnxpress.com`) and provides web hosting (`www.netans.com`) and blog installation services.

Pavel Volgarev is a software engineer with several years of experience in working with Microsoft technologies and developing for the Web. The majority of his time includes working with languages and technologies such as C#, ASP.NET MVC, RESTful Web Services, as well as HTML5-related APIs and Rich Internet Applications (RIA). He is also very keen about web design, UX, interaction design, and typography.

Prior to joining Infusion, Pavel was working as a System Architect, evolving and improving one of the finest CMS and e-commerce systems in Denmark and Europe.

Apart from being a developer, Pavel is also very passionate about blogging, public speaking, as well as startups and entrepreneurship. Pavel's complete profile is available at `http://volgarev.me`.

Table of Contents

Preface

ASP.NET Web API is a light-weight, web-based architecture that you can use to build web services that use HTTP as the protocol. This book is a clear and concise guide to the ASP.NET Web API Framework, with plenty code examples. It explores ways to consume Web API services using ASP.NET 4.5, ASP.NET MVC 4, WPF, and Silverlight clients.

What this book covers

Chapter 1, Understanding Representational State Transfer Services, provides an introduction to the concept of REST and its related terminologies.

Chapter 2, Understanding Resource and Service Oriented Architectures, explores Resource Oriented Architectures and discusses the differences between ROA and SOA.

Chapter 3, Working with Restful Services, discusses the basics of implementing RESTful services in .NET and the necessary tips and techniques.

Chapter 4, Consuming Restful Services, discusses how RESTful services can be consumed. It also discusses the guidelines and best practices involved.

Chapter 5, Working with ASP.NET 4.5, discusses how we can work with ASP.NET 4.5 and the Web API.

Chapter 6, Working with Restful Data Using Silverlight, discusses how we can work with RESTful services with Silverlight client.

Chapter 7, Advanced Features, discusses some advanced concepts in the Web API and the best practices to be followed when using WCF and ASP.NET Web API.

Appendix, Library References, discusses the popular REST-based Service Frameworks and APIs, how we can get started using Visual Studio 2013 IDE, and contains a reference to the Web API class library.

What you need for this book

- Visual Studio 2013
- SQL Server 2008 R2 / SQL Server 2012

Who this book is for

This book is for professionals who would like to build scalable REST-based services using the .NET 4.5 Framework by leveraging the features and benefits of the Web API Framework.

Conventions

In this book, you will find a number of styles of text that distinguish among different kinds of information. Here are some examples of these styles, and an explanation of their meaning.

Code words in text, database table names, folder names, filenames, file extensions, pathnames, dummy URLs, user input, and Twitter handles are shown as follows: "The `Body` section of the SOAP request contains the actual XML request object that is sent."

A block of code is set as follows:

```
<SOAP: Envelope>
  <SOAP: Header>
  </SOAP: Header>
  <SOAP: Body>
  </SOAP: Body>
</SOAP: Envelope>
```

New terms and **important words** are shown in bold. Words that you see on the screen, in menus, or dialog boxes for example, appear in the text like this: "Click on the **Restart Now** button to restart your system and complete the installation of Visual Studio 2013."

> Warnings or important notes appear in a box like this.

> Tips and tricks appear like this.

Reader feedback

Feedback from our readers is always welcome. Let us know what you think about this book—what you liked or may have disliked. Reader feedback is important for us to develop titles that you really get the most out of.

To send us general feedback, simply send an e-mail to `feedback@packtpub.com`, and mention the book title via the subject of your message.

If there is a topic that you have expertise in and you are interested in either writing or contributing to a book, see our author guide on `www.packtpub.com/authors`.

Customer support

Now that you are the proud owner of a Packt book, we have a number of things to help you to get the most from your purchase.

Downloading the example code

You can download the example code files for all Packt books you have purchased from your account at `http://www.packtpub.com`. If you purchased this book elsewhere, you can visit `http://www.packtpub.com/support` and register to have the files e-mailed directly to you.

Errata

Although we have taken every care to ensure the accuracy of our content, mistakes do happen. If you find a mistake in one of our books—maybe a mistake in the text or the code—we would be grateful if you would report this to us. By doing so, you can save other readers from frustration and help us improve subsequent versions of this book. If you find any errata, please report them by visiting `http://www.packtpub.com/submit-errata`, selecting your book, clicking on the **errata submission form** link, and entering the details of your errata. Once your errata are verified, your submission will be accepted and the errata will be uploaded on our website, or added to any list of existing errata, under the Errata section of that title. Any existing errata can be viewed by selecting your title from `http://www.packtpub.com/support`.

Piracy

Piracy of copyright material on the Internet is an ongoing problem across all media. At Packt, we take the protection of our copyright and licenses very seriously. If you come across any illegal copies of our works, in any form, on the Internet, please provide us with the location address or website name immediately so that we can pursue a remedy.

Please contact us at `copyright@packtpub.com` with a link to the suspected pirated material.

We appreciate your help in protecting our authors, and our ability to bring you valuable content.

Questions

You can contact us at `questions@packtpub.com` if you are having a problem with any aspect of the book, and we will do our best to address it.

1
Understanding Representational State Transfer Services

Representational State Transfer (**REST**) is an architecture style that is used for creating scalable services. A RESTful Web Service is one that conforms to the REST architecture constraints. The REST architectural style has quickly become very popular over the world for designing and architecting applications that can communicate. Due to its simplicity, it has gained widespread acceptance worldwide in lieu of the SOAP- and WSDL-based Web Services. It is essentially a client-server architecture and uses the stateless HTTP protocol. In this book, we will cover REST using the HTTP protocol. Our journey towards mastering REST and Web API has just begun!

In this chapter, we will cover the following topics:

- REST
- Resources and URI
- REST and RPC
- Implementing RESTful services in .NET 4.5
- Creating a WCF service
- Making the WCF service RESTful
- Specifying the binding information
- Hosting the service
- Returning the JSON data
- Consuming the RESTful service

Understanding REST

What is REST? Why is it becoming so popular over time? Is REST an alternative to Web Services? How can I make use of the .NET Framework to implement RESTful services? We will answer these questions as we progress through the sections of this chapter.

REST is an architectural style for designing distributed applications that can intercommunicate. Note that REST is not a technology or a set of standards. Rather, it is a set of constraints that can be used to define a new style of architecture. Essentially, it is a client-server architectural style where the connections are stateless.

> Note that the REST architecture style can be applied to other protocols as well. The word "stateless" implies the HTTP/HTTPS protocols. The REST architectural style is popular in the HTTP world and gives better results when used in combination with the HTTP protocol.

REST is not a standard; rather, it is an architectural alternative to RPC and Web Services. In the REST architectural style, you can communicate among systems using the HTTP protocol (if HTTP is the protocol in use). Actually, the **World Wide Web (WWW)** can be viewed as a REST-based architecture. A RESTful architecture is based on a cacheable and stateless communication protocol.

REST is an architectural style that divides an application's state and functionality into resources. These resources are in turn addressable using URIs over HTTP. These resources have a common interface and are uniquely addressable. A REST-based model is stateless, client-server-based, and cacheable.

As discussed, in a REST-based model, resources are used to represent state and functionality. Resources are identified through logical URLs. In a typical REST-based model, the client and the server communicate using requests and responses. The client sends a request to the server for a resource and the server in turn sends the response back to the client.

The main design goals of the REST architectural style include:

- Independent deployment of the components
- Reduced latency
- High security of service interactions
- Scalability
- High performance

The basic difference between SOAP and REST is that while the former emphasizes verbs, the latter emphasizes resources. In REST, you define resources, and then use a uniform interface to operate on them using the HTTP verbs. It should also be noted that REST is simpler to use, because it heavily leverages the HTTP transport mechanism for formatting, caching, routing, and operations performed on the given resources. On the contrary, with SOAP, there are no such conventions. A SOAP-based service can easily be exposed via TCP/IP, UDP, SMTP, or any other transport protocol. So, it doesn't have to be dependent on the HTTP protocol.

In a REST-based model, a request is comprised of an endpoint URL, a developer ID, parameters, and the desired action. The endpoint URL is used to represent the complete address. The developer ID is a key which uniquely identifies each request origin. The desired action is used to denote the action to be performed.

The REST architecture makes use of some common HTTP methods for **CRUD** (**Create, Read, Update, and Delete**) operations. These are as follows:

- `GET`: This is used to request for a specific representation of a resource.
- `HEAD`: This is used to retrieve the resource headers only.
- `PUT`: This is used to update a resource.
- `DELETE`: This is used to delete the specified resource.
- `POST`: This is used to submit data that is to be processed by the identified resource. Ideally, `POST` should be used for only creating resources, while `PUT` is used for only updating them.

Resources in REST-based architecture

The resource concept is one of the most important ones in REST. A few examples of public implementations of REST include the following:

- Google Fusion Tables
- Sones GraphDB: A graph-oriented database written in C#
- Nuxeo: An open-source document manager

A resource is identified using a URI. In the REST style of architecture, communication between a server and a client takes place using requests and responses. The client (also known as the consumer) requests for a resource from the server. The server then sends the response back to the client.

In the REST architectural paradigm, resources are used to represent the state and functionality of the resources. They are identified by using logical URIs so that they can be universally addressable. The REST architecture is essentially based on HTTP—a stateless protocol. However , resources can be cached as and when required. Note that since HTTP provides cache mechanism, REST implemented on top of the HTTP protocol provides the features and benefits of HTTP. Also, you can set cache expiration policies for the cached data.

Any REST request comprises of the following components:

- **An endpoint URL**: This denotes the complete address of the script.
- **Developer ID**: This is a key that is sent with each request. This is used to identify the origin of the request. Note that the developer ID is not required for all REST services.
- **Parameters**: This denotes the parameters of the request. This is optional.
- **Desired action**: This denotes the action for the particular request. Actions are based on the HTTP verbs.

Let's take an example. The following link is a typical REST request URL: `http://localhost/payroll?devkey=1&action=search&type=department&keyword=DepartmentID`.

In the previous request, the endpoint is `http://localhost/payroll`, the desired action is `search` and the developer key is `1`. You also have the `type` and `keyword` parameters provided in the request. Please refer to the following code snippet, which shows how a REST request and response looks like:

```
<?xml version="1.0" encoding=" UTF-8"?>
<Request>
<RequestId>1R3ABC</RequestId>
<Parameters>
<Argument Name="devkey" Value="1" />
<Argument Name="action" Value="search" />
<Argument Name="type" Value="department" />
<Argument Name="keyword" Value="phone" />
</Parameters>
</Request>
<Response>
<ResultCount>2</ResultCount>
<Record>
<FirstName>Joe</FirstName>
<LastName>Stagner</LastName>
<DepartmentID>1</DepartmentID>
```

```
</Record>
<Record>
<FirstName>Stephen</FirstName>
<LastName>Smith</LastName>
<DepartmentID>1</DepartmentID>
</Record>
</Response>
```

The REST architectural constraints

The REST architectural paradigm defines the following constraints to the architecture:

Client-server

A RESTful implementation is based on a client-server model. The servers and the clients are clearly isolated. This implies that the servers and clients can be modified independently. The server is not at all concerned with the user interface. Similarly, the user interface is not concerned about how data is persisted.

Stateless

The REST architecture is based on the stateless HTTP protocol. In a RESTful architecture, the server responses can be cached by the clients. Any request from the client to the server should have enough information so that the request can be understood and serviced, but no client context would be stored in the server. This type of design ensures that the servers are more visible for performance monitoring and are scalable.

Cacheable

In a typical REST architecture, the clients should be able to cache data. To manage cache better, the architecture allows us to set whether a response can be cached or not. This feature improves scalability and performance.

Code on demand

The servers in a REST architecture can (if needed) extend or customize the functionality of a particular client. This is known as "code on demand"; this feature allows the servers in a REST architecture implementation to transfer logic to the clients if such a need arises.

Uniform interface

The REST architectural style defines a uniform interface between the clients and the servers; therefore, it allows only a limited set of operations that are defined using the standard HTTP verbs, such as, `GET`, `PUT`, `POST`, and `DELETE`.

Resource management

Resource is the most important concept in the REST style architecture. Resources are identified using unique URIs. Note that resource representations can exist in any combination of any digital format (HTML, XML, JSON, RSS, and so on).

> It should be noted here that the actual resource usually has only one representation on the server. It is the client who specifies in which representation it will accept the resources; that is, how they should be formatted.

SOAP, REST, and XML-RPC – a closer look

Simple Object Access Protocol (**SOAP**) is a simple, light weight, stateless, XML-based protocol that can be used for exchangeing data between heterogeneous systems in a distributed environment. SOAP can be used to transfer data, irrespective of the platform and language in use. A typical SOAP message format is as follows:

```
<SOAP: Envelope>
  <SOAP: Header>
  </SOAP: Header>
  <SOAP: Body>
  </SOAP: Body>
</SOAP: Envelope>
```

The following code is an example of a SOAP request:

```
<?xml version="1.0" encoding="UTF-8"?>
<soapenv:Envelope
  xmlns:soapenv="http://schemas.xmlsoap.org/soap/envelope/"
  xmlns:xsd="http://www.w3.org/2001/XMLSchema"
  xmlns:xsi="http://www.w3.org/2001/XMLSchema-instance">
  <soapenv:Header>
    <ns1:RequestHeader
      soapenv:actor="http://schemas.xmlsoap.org/soap/actor/next"
      soapenv:mustUnderstand="0"
      xmlns:ns1="https://www.example.com/getData/P007">
```

```
    <ns1:authentication xsi:type="ns1:ClientLogin"
      xmlns:xsd="http://www.w3.org/2001/XMLSchema">
      <ns1:token>SuchALongToken</ns1:token>
    </ns1:authentication>
      <ns1:networkCode>ABC-XYZ-0012345</ns1:networkCode>
      <ns1:applicationName>Sample</ns1:applicationName>
    </ns1:RequestHeader>
  </soapenv:Header>
  <soapenv:Body>
    <getProductData xmlns="https://www.example.com/getData/P007">
      <filterData>
        <query>WHERE productId IS NOT NULL</query>
      </filterData>
    </getProductData>
  </soapenv:Body>
</soapenv:Envelope>
```

The following code snippet illustrates the SOAP response for the previous request:

```
<soap:Envelope xmlns:soap=
  "http://schemas.xmlsoap.org/soap/envelope/">
  <soap:Header>
    <ResponseHeader xmlns="https://www.example.com/getData/P007">
      <requestId>Some Request Id</requestId>
      <responseTime>26</responseTime>
    </ResponseHeader>
  </soap:Header>
  <soap:Body>
    <getProductDataResponse xmlns=
      "https://www.example.com/getData/P007">
      <rval>
        <totalResultSetSize>1</totalResultSetSize>
        <startIndex>0</startIndex>
        <results>
          <productId>7</productId>
          <productName>CTV</productName>
          <description>Samsung LED Color Television</description>
          <status>Active</status>
          <productCode>P007</productCode>
        </results>
      </rval>
    </getProductDataResponse>
  </soap:Body>
</soap:Envelope>
```

Note that SOAP can be used without the HTTP protocol, and SOAP always uses the `POST` operation. SOAP makes use of XML and the stateless HTTP protocol (if used with HTTP) to access services. A typical SOAP request looks like the following code:

```
GET /price HTTP/1.1
Host: http://localhost
<?xml version="1.0"?>
<soap:Envelope xmlns:soap="http://www.w3.org/2001/
  12/soap-envelope"
  xmlns:m="http://localhost/product">
  <soap:Header>
    <m:DeveloperKey>1</t>
  </soap:Header>
  <soap:Body>
    <m:GetProductPrice>
      <m:ProductCode>P001</m:ProductCode>
    </m:GetProductPrice>
</soap:Body>
</soap:Envelope>
```

In reference to the previous code snippet, the `Body` section of the SOAP request contains the actual XML request object that is sent. The following code snippet illustrates a typical SOAP response:

```
HTTP/1.1 200 OK
<?xml version="1.0"?>
<soap:Envelope xmlns:soap="http://www.w3.org/2001/
  12/soap-envelope"
  xmlns:m="http://localhost/product">
  <soap:Body>
    <m:GetProductPriceResponse>
      <m:Price>1008.78</m:Price>
    </m:GetProductPriceResponse>
  </soap:Body>
</soap:Envelope>
```

REST is an architectural paradigm that is used to model how data is represented, accessed, and modified on the Web. REST uses the stateless HTTP protocol and the standard HTTP operations (`GET`, `PUT`, `POST`, and `DELETE`) to perform CRUD operations. REST allows you to do all that you can do with SOAP and XML-RPC. Along with that, you can use firewalls for security and also use caching for enhanced performance. The REST counterpart for the same request is simple, and is shown as follows:

```
GET /product?ProductCode=P001 HTTP/1.1
Host: http://localhost
```

The REST response to the previous request would be as simple. It is shown in the following code snippet:

```
HTTP/1.1 200 OK
<?xml version="1.0"?><m:Price xmlns:m=
  "http://localhost/product">1008.78</m:Price>
```

XML-RPC is a XML-based remote procedure calling protocol. The following code snippet is an example of a typical XML-RPC POST request:

```
POST /product HTTP/1.1
Host: http://localhost
<?xml version="1.0"?>
<methodCall>
  <methodName>product.GetProductPrice</methodName>
  <params>
    <param>
      <value><string>P001</string></value>
    </param>
  </params>
</methodCall>
```

In response to the previous XML-RPC request, the following code snippet is how a typical XML-RPC response would look:

```
HTTP/1.1 200 OK
<?xml version="1.0"?>
<methodCall>
   <methodName>product.GetProductPrice</methodName>
   <params>
      <param>
         <value><double>1008.78</double></value>
      </param>
   </params>
</methodCall>
```

Understanding Windows Communication Foundation

Windows Communication Foundation (**WCF**) is a Microsoft framework that provides a unification of distributing technologies (Web Services, Remoting, COM+, and so on) under a single umbrella. The WCF Framework was first introduced in 2006 as part of the .NET Framework 3.0. It is a framework comprised of a number of technologies to provide a platform for designing applications that are based on SOA and have the capability to intercommunicate. According to Microsoft, at `http://msdn.microsoft.com/en-us/library/bb907578.aspx`,

> *Windows Communication Foundation (WCF) is a unified framework for creating secure, reliable, transacted, and interoperable distributed applications. In earlier versions of Visual Studio, there were several technologies that could be used for communicating between applications.*

The three most important concepts related to the WCF architecture include services, clients, and messages. The following figure examines the building blocks of the WCF architecture.

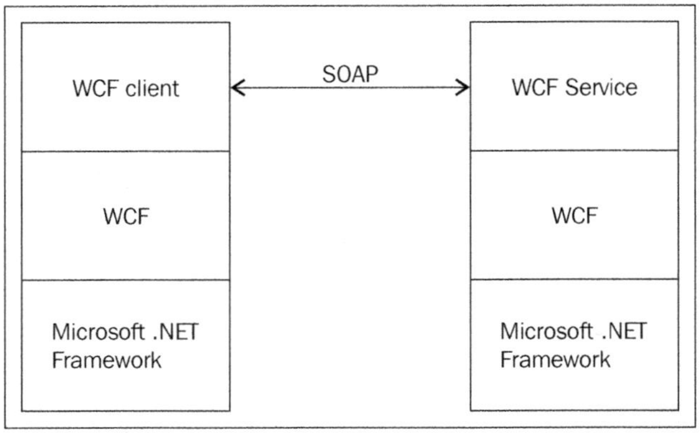

The WCF and .NET framework

The three most important concepts related to the WCF architecture are: services, clients, and messages. Contracts in the WCF can be of three types: service contract, data contract, and message contract.

WCF works on a contract-based approach. A WCF `Service` class is one that implements at least one service contract. A service contract is an interface that is used to define the operations that are exposed by the WCF `Service` class. A WCF `Service` class is just like any other .NET class, except that it is marked with the `ServiceContract` attribute. A message contract may be defined as a way that allows you to change the format of the messages. Note that the `ServiceContract`, `DataContract`, and other related attributes are defined in the `System.ServiceModel` namespace. Binding in WCF is used to specify how a particular service would communicate with other services of its kind and/or with other clients (also known as consumers).

Also, any method that is preceded by the `OperationContract` attribute is externally visible to the clients for SOAP-callable operations. If you have a method that doesn't have this attribute set, the method would not be included in the service contract, and so the WCF client would not be able to access that operation of the WCF service.

The following is a list of the pre-defined, built-in bindings in the WCF:

- BasicHttpBinding
- MsmqIntergrationBinding
- WSHttpBinding
- WSDualHttpBinding
- WSFederationHttpBinding
- NetTcpBinding
- NetNamedPipeBinding
- NetMsmqBinding
- NetPeerTcpBinding

Endpoints in the WCF are used to associate a service contract with its address. Channels are actually a bridge between the service and its client. The following types of supported channels are available in the WCF:

- Simplex Input
- Simplex Output
- Request-Reply
- Duplex

Note that a WCF service is based on three concepts: address, binding, and contract. Also, a WCF service and a WCF client communicate using messages. The following figure examines how messages are used for communication in the WCF:

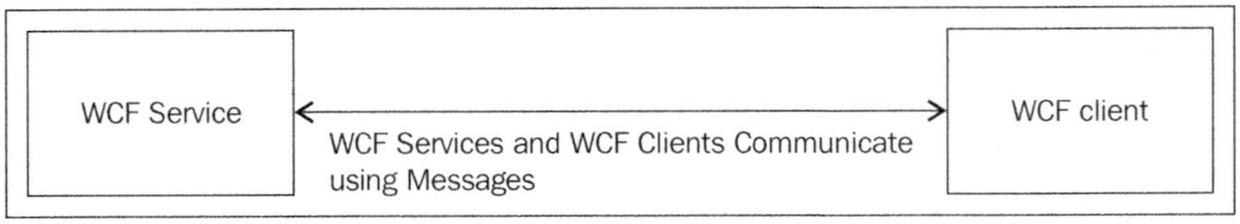

Communication in the WCF

These messages can, in turn, have one of the following patterns:

- Simplex
- Request-Reply
- Duplex

WCF 4.5 comes with improved support for REST-based features. In this section we will first implement a simple WCF service, and then make the necessary changes to it make the service RESTful. The newer versions of the WCF provide improved support for REST-based features.

REST attributes

Now, let's take a closer look at the WCF REST attributes and their purposes. Incidentally, all these attributes are available in the `System.ServiceModel.Web.dll` library. In this section, we will discuss the attributes of which we would frequently make use while working with RESTful services.

WebServiceHost

The usage of the `WebServiceHost` attribute simplifies hosting of web-based services. It derives from the `ServiceHost` class and overrides the `OnOpening` method and automatically adds the `WebHttpBehavior` class to the endpoint. The following code snippet illustrates how the `WebServiceHost` attribute is used:

```
WebServiceHost host = new WebServiceHost(typeof(ClassName),
  baseAddress);
WebHttpBinding binding = new WebHttpBinding();
host.AddServiceEndpoint(typeof(ISomeContract),
  binding, "WebServiceHost");
host.Open();
```

WebHttpBinding

The `WebHttpBinding` attribute produces an appropriate HTTP-based transport channel. Here, the security is handled by the `WebHttpSecurity` class. Services can be exposed using the `WebHttpBinding` binding by using either the `WebGet` attribute or the `WebInvoke` attribute.

The following code snippet illustrates how the `webHttpBinding` attribute is used:

```
<configuration>
  <system.serviceModel>
    <services>
      <service name="PacktService">
        <endpoint binding="webHttpBinding"
          contract="PacktService"
        behaviorConfiguration="webHttp"/>
      </service>
    </services>
    <behaviors>
      <endpointBehaviors>
        <behavior name="webHttp">
          <webHttp/>
        </behavior>
      </endpointBehaviors>
    </behaviors>
  </system.serviceModel>
<configuration>
```

WebHttpBehavior

The `WebHttpBehavior` attribute customizes the HTTP-based dispatching logic, and it overrides operation selection, serialization, and invocation. The `WebHttpBehavior` class in the `System.ServiceModel.Description` namespace is shown as follows:

```
public class WebHttpBehavior : IEndpointBehavior
{
  // Properties
  public virtual bool AutomaticFormatSelectionEnabled {
    get; set; }
  public virtual WebMessageBodyStyle DefaultBodyStyle {
    get; set; }
  public virtual WebMessageFormat DefaultOutgoingRequestFormat {
    get; set; }
  public virtual WebMessageFormat DefaultOutgoingResponseFormat {
    get; set; }
  public virtual bool FaultExceptionEnabled { get; set; }
```

```
    public virtual bool HelpEnabled { get; set; }
    protected internal string JavascriptCallbackParameterName {
      get; set; }
    // Methods
    public virtual void AddBindingParameters(ServiceEndpoint
      endpoint, BindingParameterCollection bindingParameters);
    protected virtual void AddClientErrorInspector(ServiceEndpoint
      endpoint, ClientRuntime clientRuntime);
    protected virtual void AddServerErrorHandlers(ServiceEndpoint
      endpoint, EndpointDispatcher endpointDispatcher);
    public virtual void ApplyClientBehavior(ServiceEndpoint
      endpoint, ClientRuntime clientRuntime);
    public virtual void ApplyDispatchBehavior(ServiceEndpoint
      endpoint, EndpointDispatcher endpointDispatcher);
    protected virtual WebHttpDispatchOperationSelector
      GetOperationSelector(ServiceEndpoint endpoint);
    protected virtual QueryStringConverter
      GetQueryStringConverter(OperationDescription
      operationDescription);
    protected virtual IClientMessageFormatter
      GetReplyClientFormatter(OperationDescription
      operationDescription, ServiceEndpoint endpoint);
    protected virtual IDispatchMessageFormatter
      GetReplyDispatchFormatter(OperationDescription
      operationDescription, ServiceEndpoint endpoint);
    protected virtual IClientMessageFormatter
      GetRequestClientFormatter(OperationDescription
      operationDescription, ServiceEndpoint endpoint);
    protected virtual IDispatchMessageFormatter
      GetRequestDispatchFormatter(OperationDescription
      operationDescription, ServiceEndpoint endpoint);
    public virtual void Validate(ServiceEndpoint endpoint);
    protected virtual void ValidateBinding(ServiceEndpoint
      endpoint);
}
```

WebOperationContext

The `WebOperationContext` attribute is used to access the HTTP specifics within methods. You can retrieve the current context using the `WebOperationContext.Current` property. It provides properties for incoming/outgoing request/response context.

The following code snippet illustrates how to get the HTTP status code:

```
HttpStatusCode status = WebOperationContext.
  Current.IncomingResponse.StatusCode;
```

WebMessageFormat

This attribute is used to control the message format in your services.

> Note that the WCF provides support for two primary web formats: XML and JSON.

You can control the format of your messages using the `RequestFormat` and `ResponseFormat` properties, as shown in the following code:

```
[OperationContract]
[WebGet(ResponseFormat = WebMessageFormat.Json, BodyStyle =
  WebMessageBodyStyle.WrappedRequest)]
public Employee GetData()
{
  return new Employee
  {
    Firstname = "Joydip",
    Lastname = "Kanjilal",
    Email = "joydipkanjilal@yahoo.com";
  };
}
```

WebGet

The `WebGet` attribute exposes operations using the `GET` verb. In other words, the `WebGet` attribute is used to map the incoming HTTP `GET` requests to particular WCF operations by using URI mapping. How this attribute is defined in the `System.ServiceModel.Web` namespace is shown in the following code snippet:

```
[AttributeUsageAttribute(AttributeTargets.Method)]
public sealed class WebGetAttribute : Attribute,
  IOperationBehavior
```

An example that illustrates how you can use the `WebGet` attribute is shown as follows:

```
[OperationContract]
  [WebGet(UriTemplate="/employee/{id}")]
  public Employee GetEmployee(int id)
  {
    Employee empObj = null;
    // Get employee object from the database
    return empObj;
  }
```

WebInvoke

The `WebInvoke` attribute exposes services that use other HTTP verbs, such as `POST`, `PUT`, and `DELETE`. In other words, the `WebInvoke` attribute is used for all the other HTTP verbs other than the `GET` requests. The following code snippet shows how this attribute is defined in the `System.ServiceModel.Web` namespace:

```
[AttributeUsageAttribute(AttributeTargets.Method)]
public sealed class WebInvokeAttribute : Attribute,
  IOperationBehavior
Here is an example that illustrates the usage of the WebInvoke
attribute:
[OperationContract]
  [WebInvoke(Method = "DELETE", UriTemplate = "/employee/{id}")]
  public void DeleteEmployee(int id)
  {
    // Code to delete an employee record in the database
  }
```

UriTemplate

The `UriTemplate` class belongs to `System.UriTemplate` and implements the URI template syntax that enables you to specify variables in the URI space. `UriTemplate` is a class that represents a URI template. `UriTemplate` is a URI string that contains variables enclosed by braces ({, }). Note that the `UriTemplate` property is specified on the `WebGet` and `WebInvoke` attributes that we used earlier to identify an employee resource.

The following code snippet illustrates how `UriTemplate` is used:

```
[WebGet(UriTemplate =
  "RetrieveUserDetails/{userCode}/{projectCode}")]
public string RetrieveUserDetails(string userCode,
  string projectCode)
  {

  }
```

The following table lists the important HTTP methods and their uses:

Method	Description
`GET`	This is used to request for a representation of a specific resource
`PUT`	This is used to create or update a resource with a specific representation
`DELETE`	This is used to delete a specific resource
`POST`	This is used to submit data that is to be processed by a particular resource
`HEAD`	This is similar to GET, but it retrieves only the headers

The HTTP protocol also defines a list of standard status codes that are used to specify the result of processing of a particular request. The following table lists the standard HTTP status codes and their uses:

Status Code	Description
100	Informational
200	Successful
201	Created
202	Accepted
300	Redirection
304	Not modified
400	Client error
402	Payment required
404	Not found
405	Method not allowed
500	Server error
501	Not implemented

REST-based web services

A RESTful web service (or the RESTful Web API) is a service that comprises a collection of resources. These resources include a base URI that is used to access the web service, a MIME type (that is, JSON, XML, and so on), and a set of defined operations (that is, `POST`, `GET`, `PUT`, or `DELETE`). A RESTful service is platform and language neutral. However, unlike a Web Service, there isn't any official standard set for RESTful services. REST is just an architectural style; it is devoid of any standards as such. The basic advantages of using REST are transport neutrality and the facility to use advanced `WS-*` protocols. REST is interoperable, simple to use, and has a uniform interface.

Learning RESTful web services

RESTful web services are services that are based on the REST architectural paradigm. Essentially, these (also known as a RESTful Web API) are web services that are comprised of a collection of resources. These resources are given as follows:

- A base URI used to access the web service
- A MIME type, which defines the format of the data that the web service supports, that is, JSON, XML, and so on

- A set of operations that the web service supports using the HTTP methods that include `POST`, `GET`, `PUT`, or `DELETE`

Similar to web services, a REST service is platform and language independent, based on HTTP, and can be used even with firewalls. Note that unlike web services that are based on the SOAP protocol, there is no official standard for RESTful services. REST is simply an architectural style that doesn't have any set standards. The following code snippet illustrates an example of a SOAP request:

```
<?xml version = "1.0"?>
<soap:Envelope>
xmlns:soap="http://www.w3.org/2001/12/soap-envelope"
soap:encodingStyle="http://www.w3.org/2001/12/soap-encoding">
  <soap:body emp="http://localhost/payroll">
    <emp:GetEmployeeDetails>
       <emp:EmployeeID>1</emp:EmployeeID>
    </emp:GetEmployeeDetails>
  </soap:Body>
</soap:Envelope>
```

The following URLshows how the same can be represented using REST:

```
http://localhost/payroll/EmployeeDetails/1
```

The RESTful web services map the HTTP methods to the corresponding CRUD operations. The previous two tables show how these are mapped:

- HTTP Method: CRUD Action
- GET: Retrieve a resource
- POST: Create a new resource
- PUT: Update an existing resource
- DELETE: Delete an existing resource
- HEAD: Retrieves metadata information on a resource

Implementing RESTful services in .NET 4.5

In this section, we will implement a RESTful service using the WCF. The WCF is a framework based on the **Service Oriented Architecture** (**SOA**) that is used to design distributed applications, which are applications that have the capability to intercommunicate. We will explore more about the WCF in *Chapter 3, Working with Restful Services.*

The UserNamePasswordValidator class

The `UserNamePasswordValidator` class has been introduced in the newer versions of the WCF. You can use this class to design and implement your own custom validators for validating a user's credentials.

The `UserNamePasswordValidator` class in the `System.IdentityModel.Selectors` namespace can be used to validate user credentials in WCF 4.5. You can create your own custom validator by simply extending the `UserNamePasswordValidator` class, and then overriding the `Validate` method, as shown in the following code snippet:

```
using System;
using System.IdentityModel.Selectors;
using System.IdentityModel.Tokens;
using System.ServiceModel;
namespace Packt
{
  public class PacktValidator : UserNamePasswordValidator
  {
    public override void Validate(String userName,
      String password)
    {
      if (!userName.Equals("joydip")) ||
        !password.Equals("joydip1@3"))
      {
        throw new SecurityTokenException("User Name and/or
        Password incorrect...!");
      }
    }
  }
}
```

Then, you can configure the validator you just created in the configuration file, as shown in the following code:

```
<?xml version="1.0" encoding="utf-8" ?>
<configuration>
  <system.web>
    <compilation debug="true" />
  </system.web>
  <system.serviceModel>
    <services>
      <bindings>
        <wsHttpBinding>
          <binding name="PacktAuthentication">
            <security mode="Transport">
```

```
                <transport clientCredentialType="Basic" />
              </security>
            </binding>
          </wsHttpBinding>
        </bindings>

        <behaviors>
          <serviceBehaviors>
            <behavior name="PacktValidator.ServiceBehavior">
              <serviceCredentials>
                <userNameAuthentication
                userNamePasswordValidationMode="Custom"
                customUserNamePasswordValidatorType="Packt.
                PacktValidator, Packt"/>
              </serviceCredentials>
            </behavior>
          </serviceBehaviors>
        </behaviors>
      </services>
    </system.serviceModel>
  </configuration>
```

The new enhancements in WCF 4.5 include the following:

- Simplified configuration
- Standard endpoints
- Discovery
- Simplified IIS Hosting
- REST improvements
- Workflow services
- Routing service
- Automatic Help page

Simplified configuration

WCF 4.5 starts with the default configuration model. The configuration in WCF 4.5 is much simpler in comparison with its earlier counterparts. In WCF 3.x, you needed to specify the endpoints, behavior, and so on for the service host. With WCF 4.5, default endpoints, binding information, and behavior are provided. In essence, WCF 4.0 eliminates the need of any WCF configuration when you are implementing a particular WCF service.

There are a few standard endpoints and default binding/behavior configurations that are created for any WCF service in WCF 4.5. This makes it easy to get started with the WCF, because the tedious configuration details of WCF 3.x are no longer required.

Consider the following WCF service:

```
using System;
using System.ServiceModel;
namespace PacktService
{
  [ServiceContract]
  public interface ITestService
  {
    [OperationContract]
    String DisplayMessage();
  }

  public class TestService : ITestService
  {
    public String DisplayMessage()
    {
      return "Hello World!";
    }
  }
}
```

In WCF 4.5, you can use `ServiceHost` to host the WCF service without the need for any configuration information whatsoever. The following code is all that you need to host your WCF service and display the address, binding, and contract information:

```
using System.ServiceModel;
using System;
using System.ServiceModel.Description;
namespace PacktClient
{
  class Program
  {
    static void Main(string[] args)
    {
      ServiceHost serviceHost = new ServiceHost
        (typeof(PacktService.TestService));
      serviceHost.AddServiceEndpoint
        (typeof(PacktService.TestService),
        new BasicHttpBinding(),
        "http://localhost:1607/
        TestService.svc");
```

```
            serviceHost.Open();
            foreach (ServiceEndpoint serviceEndpoint
              in serviceHost.Description.Endpoints)
            Console.WriteLine("Address: {0}, Binding: {1},
              Contract: {2}", serviceEndpoint.Address,
              serviceEndpoint.Binding.Name,
              serviceEndpoint.Contract.Name);
            Console.ReadLine();
            serviceHost.Close();
        }
    }
}
```

The following code is an example of all the configuration information that you need to specify to consume your service in WCF 4.5:

```
<?xml version="1.0" encoding="utf-8" ?>
<configuration>
  <system.serviceModel>
    <behaviors>
      <serviceBehaviors>
        <behavior>
          <serviceMetadata httpGetEnabled ="true"/>
        </behavior>
      </serviceBehaviors>
    </behaviors>
  </system.serviceModel>
</configuration>
```

Note that the `BasicHttpBinding` binding used is by default. If you want to choose a more secure binding, such as `WSHttpBinding`, you can change the binding information by using the following code snippet:

```
<?xml version="1.0" encoding="utf-8" ?>
<configuration>
  <system.serviceModel>
    <behaviors>
      <serviceBehaviors>
        <behavior>
          <serviceMetadata httpGetEnabled ="true"/>
        </behavior>
      </serviceBehaviors>
    </behaviors>
    <protocolMapping>
      <add binding="wsHttpBinding" scheme ="http"/>
    </protocolMapping>
  </system.serviceModel>
</configuration>
```

Standard endpoints

Standard endpoints are preconfigured endpoints in the WCF Framework 4.5. You can always re-use them, but they don't generally change.

You can use any of the previous endpoints by referencing them in the `<configuration>` element using the endpoint name. An example of the same is given as follows:

```
<configuration>
  <system.serviceModel>
    <services>
      <service name="PacktService">
        <endpoint kind="basicHttpBinding" contract="IMyService"/>
        <endpoint kind="mexEndpoint" address="mex" />
      </service>
    </services>
  </system.serviceModel>
</configuration>
```

Discovery

There are two modes of operation. They are given as follows:

- **Ad-Hoc mode**: In this mode, there is no centralized server, and all service announcements and client requests are sent in a multicast manner.
- **Managed mode**: In this mode, you have a centralized server. Such a server is known as a discovery proxy, where the services are published centrally and the clients who need to consume such published services connect to this to retrieve the necessary information.

You can just add the standard `udpDiscoveryEndpoint` endpoint and also enable the `<serviceDiscovery>` behavior to enable service discovery in the Ad-hoc mode. The following code is an example of this:

```
<configuration>
  <system.serviceModel>
    <services>
      <service name="TestService">
        <endpoint binding="wsHttpBinding"
          contract="ITestService" />
        <!-- add a standard UDP discovery endpoint-->
        <endpoint name="udpDiscovery" kind="
          udpDiscoveryEndpoint"/>
      </service>
```

```
    </services>
    <behaviors>
      <serviceBehaviors>
        <behavior name="TestService.MyServiceBehavior">
          <!-- To avoid disclosing metadata information, set the
            value below to false and remove the metadata
            endpoint above before deployment -->
          <serviceMetadata httpGetEnabled="true"/>
            <!-- To receive exception details in
              faults for debugging
              purposes, set the value below to true. Set to false
              before deployment to avoid disclosing exception
              information -->
            <serviceDebug includeExceptionDetailInFaults="false"/>
          <serviceDiscovery />
        </behavior>
      </serviceBehaviors>
    </behaviors>
  </system.serviceModel>
</configuration>
```

Note that in the previous code snippet, a new endpoint has been added to discover the service. Also, the `ServiceDiscovery` behavior has been added. You can use the `DiscoveryClient` class to discover your service and invoke one of its methods.

You must create an instance of the `DiscoveryClient` class and pass `UdpDiscoveryEndPoint` to the constructor of this class as a parameter to discover the service. Once the endpoint has been discovered, the discovered endpoint address can then be used to invoke the service. The following code snippet illustrates this:

```
using System;
using System.ServiceModel;
using System.ServiceModel.Discovery;
namespace PacktConsoleApplication
{
  class Program
  {
    static void Main(string[] args)
    {
      DiscoveryClient discoverclient = new DiscoveryClient(new
        UdpDiscoveryEndpoint());
      FindResponse findResponse = discoverclient.Find(new
        FindCriteria(typeof(ITestService)));
      EndpointAddress endpointAddress =
        findResponse.Endpoints[0].Address;
```

```
            MyServiceClient serviceClient = new MyServiceClient(new
              WSHttpBinding(), endpointAddress);
            Console.WriteLine(serviceClient.DisplayMessage());
        }
    }
}
```

WCF 4.5 also enables you to configure services to announce their endpoints as soon as they are started. The following code shows how you can configure your service to announce endpoints at the time it starts:

```
<configuration>
  <system.serviceModel>
    <services>
      <service name="TestService">
        <endpoint binding="wsHttpBinding"
          contract="ITestService"/>
        <endpoint kind="udpDiscoveryEndpoint"/>
      </service>
    </services>
    <behaviors>
      <serviceBehaviors>
        <behavior>
          <serviceDiscovery>
            <announcementEndpoints>
              <endpoint kind="udpAnnouncementEndpoint"/>
            </announcementEndpoints>
          </serviceDiscovery>
        </behavior>
      </serviceBehaviors>
    </behaviors>
  </system.serviceModel>
</configuration>
```

Simplified IIS hosting

Hosting of WCF 4.5 applications on IIS has now become much easier. An example of a simple WCF service is given as follows:

```
<!-- PacktService.svc -->
<%@ ServiceHost Language="C#" Debug="true" Service=" PacktService
  CodeBehind="~/App_Code/PacktService.cs" %>
[ServiceContract]
public class PacktService
{
  [OperationContract]
```

```
    public string GetMessage()
    {
      return "This is a test service.";
    }
  }
```

You can then enable service metadata for the service in the application's `web.config` configuration file, as shown in the following code snippet:

```
<system.serviceModel>
  <behaviors>
    <serviceBehaviors>
      <behavior>
        <serviceMetadata httpGetEnabled="true"/>
      </behavior>
    </serviceBehaviors>
  </behaviors>
</system.serviceModel>
```

You can also define virtual service activation endpoints for your WCF 4.5 services in your application's `web.config` configuration file. By doing so, you can activate your WCF service without the need for `.svc` files. You need to specify the following configuration in your application's `web.config` configuration file to activate your service without the need for a `.svc` file:

```
<configuration>
  <system.serviceModel>
    <serviceHostingEnvironment>
      <serviceActivations>
        <add relativeAddress="PacktService.svc"
          service="PacktService"/>
      </serviceActivations>
    </serviceHostingEnvironment>
  </system.serviceModel>
</configuration>
```

Improvements in REST

WCF 4.5 comes with improved support for REST-based features. You now have support for an automatic help page that describes the REST-based services available for the service consumers or clients. This feature is turned on by default, but you can also manually configure it, as shown in the following code listing:

```
<configuration>
  <system.serviceModel>
    <serviceHostingEnvironment aspNetCompatibilityEnabled=
      "true" />
```

```
    <behaviors>
      <endpointBehaviors>
        <behavior name="PacktTestHelpBehavior">
          <webHttp helpEnabled="true" />
        </behavior>
      </endpointBehaviors>
    </behaviors>
    <services>
      <service name="PacktSampleWCFService">
        <endpoint behaviorConfiguration="PacktTestHelpBehavior"
          binding="webHttpBinding"
          contract="PacktSampleWCFService" />
      </service>
    </services>
  </system.serviceModel>
</configuration>
```

WCF 4.5 also comes with support for HTTP caching, which is done by using the `AspNetCacheProfile` attribute. Note that the `AspNetCacheProfile` support actually uses the standard ASP.NET output caching mechanism to provide you with caching features in your WCF service.

To use this attribute, you should add a reference to the `System.ServiceModel.Web.Caching` namespace. You can apply this attribute in a `WebGet` operation and specify the cache duration of your choice. The following code snippet can be used in your service contract method to make use of this feature:

```
using System.ServiceModel.Web.Caching;
[OperationContract]
[WebGet]
[AspNetCacheProfile("PacktCache")]
String GetProductName();
```

Accordingly, you should set the cache profile in your application's `web.config` file, as shown here:

```
<caching>
  <outputCacheSettings>
    <outputCacheProfiles>
      <add name="PacktCache" duration="60" varyByParam="format"/>
    </outputCacheProfiles>
  </outputCacheSettings>
</caching>
```

Implementing a RESTful Service using WCF 4.5

In this section, we will implement our first RESTful service using WCF 4.5. To do this, we need to follow these steps:

1. Create a WCF Service
2. Make the service RESTful
3. Specify binding information
4. Host the RESTful service
5. Consume the RESTful service

Creating a WCF service

A typical WCF implementation would have a WCF service and a WCF client. The WCF client would consume the services provided by the WCF service.

Note that a WCF service contains:

- A `Service` class
- A hosting environment
- One or more endpoints

The `Service` class is written using a language targeted at the managed environment of the .NET CLR. In essence, the `Service` class can be written in any .NET language of your choice (we use C# throughout this book). The hosting environment is the environment inside the context of which the WCF service would execute. The endpoints enable the clients or the service consumers to access the WCF service.

There are two templates from which you can choose to create the WCF services: the Visual Studio 2013 WCF service library template and the Visual Studio service application template.

Let's first use the Visual Studio WCF service library template to create a WCF service. To do this, follow these steps:

1. Open Visual Studio 2013 IDE
2. Navigate to **File** | **New** | **Project**

3. Select **WCF Service Application** from the list of templates displayed, as shown in the following screenshot:

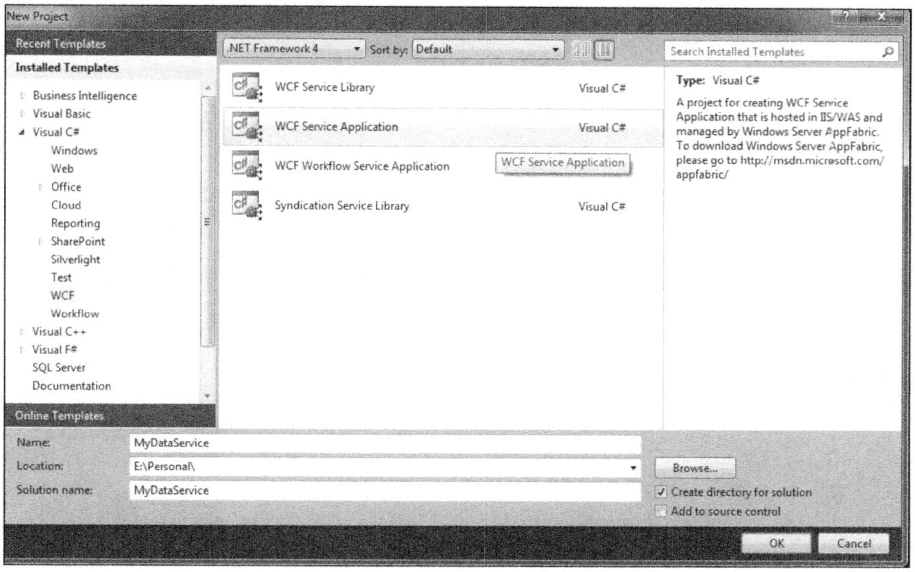

Creating a WCF Service Application Project

4. Provide a name for your project, and click on **OK** to save.

A WCF service application project is created. At first glance, the `Service` class looks like the following code:

```
using System;
namespace MyDataService
{
  // NOTE: You can use the "Rename" command on the "Refactor" menu to
change
  // the class name "Service1" in code, svc and config file together.
  public class Service1 : IService1
  {
    public string GetData(int value)
    {
      return string.Format("You entered: {0}", value);
    }

    public CompositeType GetDataUsingDataContract(
      CompositeType composite)
    {
      if (composite == null)
      {
```

```
        throw new ArgumentNullException("composite");
      }
      if (composite.BoolValue)
      {
        composite.StringValue += "Suffix";
      }
      return composite;
    }
  }
}
```

The `Service` class in the previous code snippet implements the `IService1` interface, as shown here:

```
using System.Runtime.Serialization;
using System.ServiceModel;
namespace MyDataService
{
  // NOTE: You can use the "Rename" command on the "Refactor" menu
  // to change the interface name "IService1" in both code
  // and config file together.
  [ServiceContract]
  public interface IService1
  {
    [OperationContract]
    string GetData(int value);
    [OperationContract]
    CompositeType GetDataUsingDataContract(
      CompositeType composite);
    // TODO: Add your service operations here
  }
  // Use a data contract as illustrated in the sample below
  // to add composite types to service operations.
  [DataContract]
  public class CompositeType
  {
    bool boolValue = true;
    string stringValue = "Hello ";
    [DataMember]
    public bool BoolValue
    {
      get { return boolValue; }
      set { boolValue = value; }
    }
```

```
            [DataMember]
            public string StringValue
            {
                get { return stringValue; }
                set { stringValue = value; }
            }
        }
    }
```

Consider the following WCF service:

```
    using System.ServiceModel;
    namespace Test
    {
        [ServiceContract]
        public interface ITestService
        {
            [OperationContract]
            String GetMessage();
        }
        public class TestService : ITestService
        {
            public string GetMessage()
            {
                return "Hello World!";
            }
        }
    }
```

> Note the usage of the `OperationContract` attribute in the previous code snippet. This attribute is used to specify that a particular operation is exposed to calls by clients.

To host this WCF service, you can write the following code:

```
    using System;
    using System.ServiceModel;
    using Test;
    namespace MyApp
    {
        class Program
        {
            static void Main(string[] args)
            {
```

```
            using (ServiceHost serviceHost = new
              ServiceHost(typeof(TestService)))
            {
              serviceHost.Open();
              Console.WriteLine("WCF Service has started...");
              Console.ReadLine();
              serviceHost.Close();
            }
            Console.WriteLine("The WCF Service has stopped...");
        }
      }
    }
```

Making the service RESTful

When designing a RESTful service, you need to know the resources, the URIs that would be used to map those resources, and the HTTP verbs that should be supported by the resources.

In a typical WCF-REST based service, you would need the `WebGet` attribute, apart from the `OperationContract` attribute you use to expose the operations of the service. The `WebGet` attribute belongs to the `System.ServiceModel.Web` namespace. A typical `WebGet` attribute for HTTP-GET operation is shown as follows:

```
[WebGet(UriTemplate =
"/payroll/getemployees.xml",
  BodyStyle = WebMessageBodyStyle.Bare,
  RequestFormat = WebMessageFormat.Xml,
  ResponseFormat = WebMessageFormat.Xml)]
```

The `UriTemplate` parameter of the `WebGet` attribute is used to define the URL format for accessing the service operation. The `RequestFormat` and `ResponseFormat` arguments are a part of the `WebMessageFormat` enumeration and can have one of the two possible values: `Xml` and `Json`. The following code is how a typical `WebGet` attribute for a HTTP-POST operation looks:

```
[GetOperationContract]
[WebInvoke(UriTemplate =
"/payroll/updateemployee.xml?
     employeecode={code}",
       Method = "POST",
       BodyStyle = WebMessageBodyStyle.Bare,
       RequestFormat = WebMessageFormat.Xml,
       ResponseFormat = WebMessageFormat.Xml)]
```

To make the service we created earlier in this chapter RESTful, just change the contract ITest and specify the `WebGet` attribute, as shown in the following code snippet:

```
[ServiceContract]
[WebGet()]
  public interface ITestService
  {
    [OperationContract]
    String GetMessage();
  }
```

Specifying the binding information

Now that we have created the service contract and the service, along with the operations that the service would expose, we need to specify the binding information for the service so that it can be assessable by service consumers or clients. In order for a WCF service to be accessed by the clients, the service should expose endpoints. An endpoint denotes the address, binding, and contract information for the service. To specify the binding information for the service, open the `App.Config` file and write the following code inside the `<system.serviceModel>` tag:

```
<system.serviceModel>
  <bindings>
  </bindings>
  <services>
    <service name ="Test.TestService"
      behaviorConfiguration="Default">
      <host>
        <baseAddresses>
          <add baseAddress="http://localhost:8080/Test"/>
        </baseAddresses>
      </host>
      <endpoint
        address=""
        binding ="basicHttpBinding"
        contract="Test.ITestService" />
    </service>
  </services>
  <behaviors>
    <serviceBehaviors>
      <behavior name="Default">
        <serviceMetadata httpGetEnabled="true"/>
      </behavior>
    </serviceBehaviors>
  </behaviors>
</system.serviceModel>
```

In our example, we are using a RESTful service. So, we need to use the `webHttpBinding` class, as shown here:

```
<service name ="Test.TestService" behaviorConfiguration="Default">
  <host>
    <baseAddresses>
     <add baseAddress="http://localhost:8080/Test"/>
    </baseAddresses>
  </host>
  <endpoint
    address=""
    binding ="webHttpBinding"
    contract="Test.TestService" />
</service>
```

Hosting the RESTful WCF service

There are many ways in which a WCF service can be hosted. For example, you can host your WCF service in the IIS server, or by using the **Windows Activation Service (WAS)**. To host your WCF service in IIS, you must create a virtual directory, and make it point to the directory where your service is located. Note that the WCF services hosted in IIS can be accessed using SOAP over HTTP.

What you can specify in the `App.Config` file in the hosting application to access your WCF service hosted in IIS is as follows:

```
<?xml version="1.0" encoding="utf-8" ?>
<configuration>
  <system.serviceModel>
    <behaviors>
      <serviceBehaviors>
        <behavior>
          <serviceMetadata httpGetEnabled ="true"/>
        </behavior>
      </serviceBehaviors>
    </behaviors>
    <protocolMapping>
      <add binding="wsHttpBinding" scheme ="http"/>
    </protocolMapping>
  </system.serviceModel>
</configuration>
```

Hosting the service inside the console application

You can also host your WCF service programmatically if the endpoints are properly defined. To host the RESTful WCF service we created earlier, you should use `WebServiceHost`, as shown here:

```
using System;
using System.ServiceModel;
using System.ServiceModel.Web;
using Test;
namespace MyApp
{
  class Program
  {
    static void Main(string[] args)
    {
      using (WebServiceHost serviceHost = new
        WebServiceHost(typeof(TestService)))
      {
        serviceHost.Open();
        Console.WriteLine("WCF Service has started...");
        Console.ReadLine();
        serviceHost.Close();
      }
      Console.WriteLine("The WCF Service has stopped...");
    }
  }
}
```

Returning JSON data

You can return data in **JavaScript Object Notation (JSON)** format from your REST-based WCF service. The following code snippet illustrates how you can return data from your RESTful service in a JSON format by setting the attributes:

```
using System.Xml;
using System.Text;
using System.IO;
using System.Runtime.Serialization;
using System.ServiceModel;
using System.ServiceModel.Channels;
using System.ServiceModel.Web;
namespace Test
{
```

```
    [ServiceContract]
    public interface ITestService
    {
      [OperationContract]
      [WebGet(UriTemplate = "Test")]
      Message GetMessage();
    }
    public class TestService : ITestService
    {
      public Message GetMessage()
      {
        StringBuilder stringBuilder = new StringBuilder();
        using (XmlWriter xmlWriter =
          XmlWriter.Create(stringBuilder))
        {
          xmlWriter.WriteStartDocument();
          xmlWriter.WriteStartElement("Message");
          xmlWriter.WriteAttributeString("type", "Name");
          xmlWriter.WriteString("Joydip");
          xmlWriter.WriteEndElement();
          xmlWriter.WriteEndDocument();
        }
        TextReader textReader = new
          StringReader(stringBuilder.ToString());
        XmlReader xmlReader = XmlReader.Create(textReader);
        return Message.CreateMessage(MessageVersion.None, "",
          xmlReader);
      }
    }
  }
```

Note that the `WebGet` attribute in the WCF is actually a part of the HTTP programming model for the WCF. This attribute is used to invoke the WCF service using the HTTP URI. In essence, the `WebGet` attribute is used to specify that the service would respond to the HTTP `GET` requests.

The `WebGet` attribute accepts one of the following four parameters:

- `BodyStyle`: This is used to specify whether the requests or responses should be wrapped
- `RequestFormat`: This is used to format the request messages
- `ResponseFormat`: This is used to format the response messages
- `UriTemplate`: This is used to specify the URI template for the HTTP requests for a service operation

The previous code snippet used an `XmlWriter` instance to create a message in XML format. And, here is what the returned JSON data would look like:

```
{
"Message": [
  { "Name":"Joydip"},
  ]
}
```

Consuming the RESTful Service

To consume the RESTful service we created earlier in this section, you would need to create a client application (ASP.NET or WPF), add a service reference to the service we created in the earlier sections, and then use the service reference instance to invoke the service methods. We will discuss this in detail in *Chapter 3, Working with Restful Services* and *Chapter 4, Consuming RESTful Services.*

Summary

REST is now all set to be the architectural paradigm of choice for designing and implementing scalable services. The RESTful Web Services expose resources through URIs and use the HTTP methods to perform CRUD operations. The REST architectural paradigm not only opens up a lot of possibilities, but also challenges. We will explore these as we progress through the chapters of this book. This chapter gave an introduction to REST, an architectural style for distributed hypermedia systems. In the next chapter, we will explore Resource Oriented Architectures in detail.

2

Understanding Resource and Service Oriented Architectures

Software architecture refers to the overall structure of a system and the interrelationships of entities and components that make up the system. There are various architectural styles like Object Oriented Architecture, Service Oriented Architecture, Cloud Oriented Architecture and Resource Oriented Architecture.

Service Oriented Architecture (**SOA**) and **Resource Oriented Architecture** (**ROA**) are architectural design patterns that provide the concepts and the necessary development tools and technologies for implementing distributed application architectures. Distributed architectures comprises services that can be used by the clients over a network by using well-defined interfaces. These components that are used by the clients are named resources in ROA and services in SOA.

In this chapter, we will discuss the basics of Resource Oriented Architectures and how they differ from Service Oriented and Object Oriented Architectures. We will also explore the best practices in designing and implementing ROAs.

In this chapter, we will cover the following topics:

- SOA
- ROA
- What is resource orientation?
    - Resource orientation concepts
    - Addressability
    - Statelessness
    - Representations

- Resource Oriented Services and REST
- Resource Oriented Services and web services
- Read-only and Read/Write Resource Oriented Services
- Guidelines and best practices

Understanding SOA

SOA is an architectural paradigm where you have a collection of loosely coupled and extensible services, each service having the capability to be modified independent of another in such a way that the integration of the services remain intact. SOA is composed of a collection of discrete software modules known as services. These services can exchange data and information with other services.

Note that the SOA architectural paradigm is based on functional decomposition of the business architecture of an enterprise. In doing so, it introduces two distinct high-level abstractions, that is, business services for the enterprise and business processes for the enterprise. While the business services represent the business functions of the enterprise, the business processes define the functioning of the business of the enterprise.

SOA can be implemented using one of the following technologies:

- Web services
- Windows Communication Foundation
- CORBA
- DCOM
- JINI
- EJB

SOA enables an excellent integration of loosely coupled distributed applications and services over a network. SOA is essentially a collection of services that can communicate. Note that web services, J2EE, CORBA, and so on, are actually the implementations of SOA. The most important benefits of a service-oriented design include the following:

- Platform and language independence
- Loose coupling
- Location transparency and reduced cost of maintenance
- Support for seamless updates over time
- Easier maintenance and seamless deployment

- An SOA design is comprises a number of elements, including the following:
    - Service
    - Service provider
    - Service consumer
    - Service registry
    - Service contract

Let's look at each of these in more detail.

Service

A service may be defined as an implementation of a well-defined, self-contained, and independent business functionality that has the capability of accepting one or multiple requests, and returning one or multiple responses using a well-defined standard interface. A service is independent of the technology on which it is implemented; so the interface to the service should be platform independent. A service should also have the capability to be discovered dynamically and called at runtime. A service provides business functions as service operations to the service consumer.

A service is a unit of design, implementation, and deployment artifact that is used for implementation of enterprise architectures. A service is defined using a verb. For example, validate a customer's credentials; this describes the business function it implements. A service implementation defines a service interface in either an RPC style or a messaging style. Although the former uses service invocation techniques, the latter executes a service operation as defined in the service semantics.

Service provider

The service provider is a network-addressable entity that provides the service. Note that in SOA, a service provider can also be a service consumer.

Service consumer

The service consumer is the entity that consumes (or uses) the services provided by the service provider by locating the service in the service registry, binding to the service, and then executing the service methods. A service consumer is also known as the service client or simply the client.

Service registry

The service registry is a network-based repository of published services. At runtime, this registry is used by the service consumers to locate a service and bind to it. The advantages of using a service registry includes:

- Scalability
- Loose coupling
- Hot updates
- Dynamic service lookup

Service contract

The service contract is a specification that denotes how the service consumer would interact with the service provider for a particular service. The following figure illustrates the relationship between service contract and its implementation

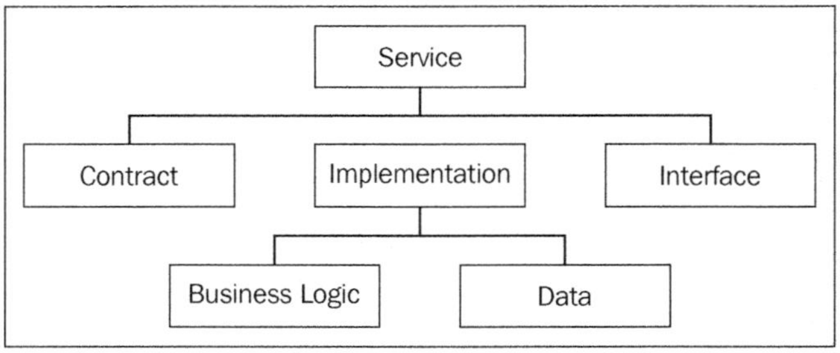

Relationship between service contract and service implementation

Service proxy

The service proxy is a reference to the service at the service consumer's end—it is provided by the service provider to facilitate the service method calls. A service consumer or service client uses this proxy to invoke one or more service methods.

Service lease

The service lease is a predefined duration that denotes the lifetime of a service. This implies a time after which the service would no longer be valid. Note that, as and when this time period elapses, the service consumer should request the service registry to grant a fresh, new service lease so that the service consumer can regain access to the service and execute the service methods.

Message

Service providers and service consumers communicate through messages. So, messages are the medium of communication between service providers (that is, the providers of the services) and service consumers (that is, the consumers of the services). Note that such messages are essentially made available in a predefined XML format. In addition to the XML format, it can also be in the JSON format or any other format upon which both the service provider and consumer mutually agreed upon. The figure given below shows that a service communicates with another through the usage of messages

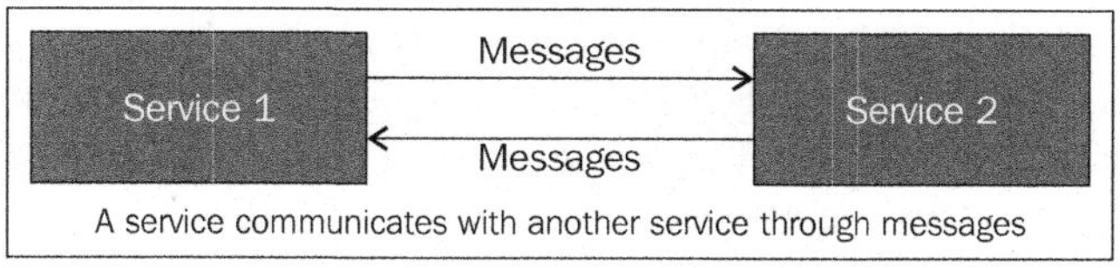

Services communicate with one another using message exchanges

Service description

The service description is a specification that contains the information that is necessary to invoke a service. Such information may include the parameters, the constraints, and the policies that define how the service should be invoked.

Advertising and discovery

Advertising and discovery are two of the most essential properties in SOA. Although the former relates to the capability of a service to publish its description so as to be located by the service consumers, the latter relates to the capability of the service consumers to discover the published services from the service registry and then invoke them as (and when) necessary.

From object orientation to SOA to ROA to REST

Call-based distributed systems have one of the following architectural styles:

- Object Oriented Architectures
- SOAs
- ROAs

Object Oriented Architectures deal with object instances, and communications are implicitly stateful. State information is stored on the server side. Each access to an object instance involves a round trip communication.

SOAs revolve around a service and the endpoint it exposes. SOAs are stateless and scalable easily because of their stateless nature. The REST architectural paradigm treats all entities in the world as connected resources and re-uses the existing HTTP infrastructure. The ability to cache requests, ability to perform stateless interactions, scalability, simplicity, agility, and flexibility are some of the benefits of this architecture. However, lack of references, lack of tools support, and lack of a proper standardization are the disadvantages of this architecture.

A service does have an interface, and can be referenced during its lifetime. It doesn't necessarily have a state. Each service has an interface description that defines the message and payload formats. A service can be discovered and dynamically bound. It is modular, self-contained, interoperable, addressable, and locatable via a network. A service can also be composed of other services. The following figure illustrates the relationship between service consumer, service provider, and a service broker.

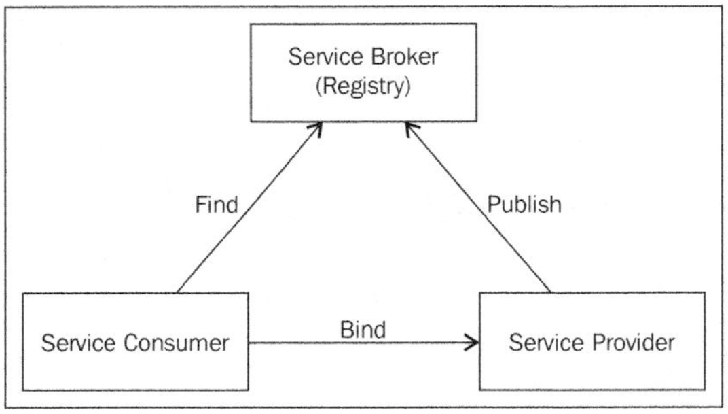

Relation between service provider, service consumer, and service broker

Services are made available to the clients (service consumers) by publishing the services in a repository named **Service Broker (Registry)**. The **Service Consumer** (service client) locates the service, uses a service proxy, and then invokes one or more service methods using the service proxy instance The following figure shows how a service consumer talks to the service registry.

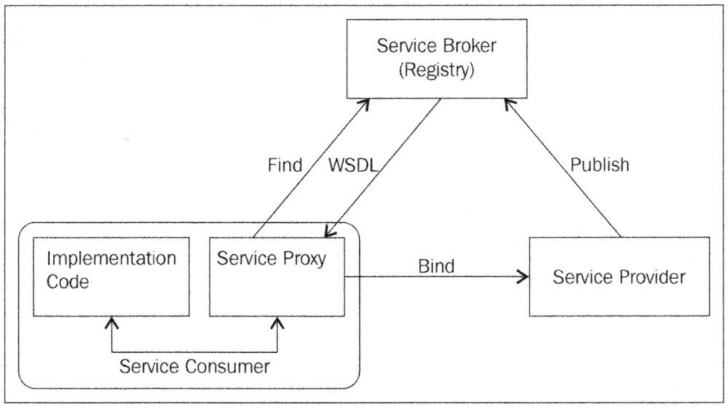

The service consumer talks to the service registry and the service provider using a service proxy

ROAs are stateless, and revolve around a resource. Each resource is identified using a URI. You can always have multiple copies of the same resource. In Resource Oriented Architecture, requests are usually stateless: there is no link among one request and the next. Resource lifecycle is managed using verbs, that is, HTTP, PUT, HTTP, DELETE, and so on.

REST services are easier to implement than SOAP-based SOA. Also, REST services provide a support for better caching, lightweight requests and responses, and reduced network traffic.

REST constraints are design rules applied to the REST architectural style. We will explore more on these design constraints in the next chapter.

These REST constraints are:

- Client-server
- Stateless
- Cache
- Interface / Uniform Contract
- Layered system
- Code-On-Demand

SOA and ROA are two distinctly different architectural paradigms. In the former, a service is what is given importance. However, in the latter, resources are given importance. So, verbs are given importance in SOA, while nouns are given importance in ROA. In ROA, the common verbs used for resource life cycle management include PUT and DELETE. We will explore this later in this book.

The key REST principles are given as follows:

- A resource should have an ID
- Link related resources
- Use standard methods
- Resources can have multiple representations
- Communicate statelessly

A look at ROA

ROA is primarily based on the concept of a resource. A resource is a distributable component that can be accessed through a standard, common interface. Each resource is associated to a unique identifier that comprises a URL.

The main concepts of ROA are centered on resources. Resources should have the following characteristics:

- A resource should be unique and maybe linked to other related resources.
- A resource should have a minimum of one representation.
- A resource should have attributes and schema, it should be accessible (through its address), and it should provide a context.
- A resource should have name; this is used to identify a resource uniquely. Resources are identified using URIs.

Although a resource link is used to represent another representation of the same resource or another resource, a resource interface is used to provide an interface to access a resource and manipulate its state information. A resource is represented using URIs. Note that data is a resource if it can be represented using a URI.

Examples of resources and URIs are as follows:

- `http://www.mysoftware.com/software/releases/1.0.0.1.zip`
- `http://www.mysoftware.com/software/releases/1.0.0.2.zip`
- `http://www.mystore.com/search/Books/NewBook`

No two resources can be the same, but two or more resources can point to the same data. Here is an example:

- `http://www.packtpub.com/sales/2012/Q4`
- `http://www.packtpub.com/sales/2012/Q3`

The following figure shows the relationship amongst a resource, its representation, and its URI:

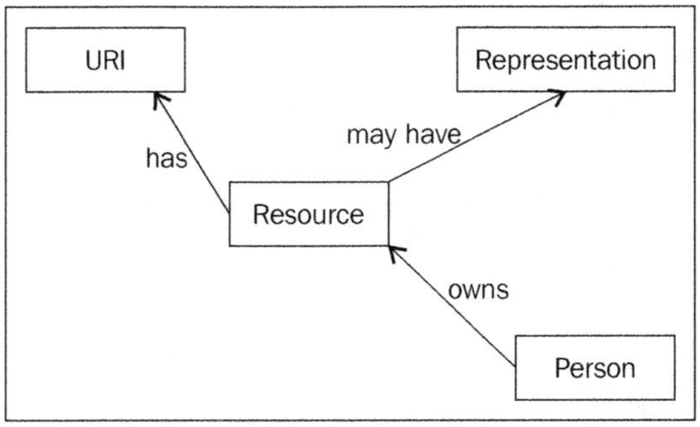

Relation between Resource, Representation, and URI

Basic properties of ROAs

The six basic properties that an ROA implementation should hold include the following:

- **Addressability**: This denotes the ability to share data and information via URIs.
- **Statelessness**: This implies that every request on a RESTful web service should be self-contained. In order to achieve this statelessness nature, all calls to a RESTful service should contain relevant bits of application state in each request.
- **Connectedness**: This implies that resources should contain links to related resources.
- **Representation**: A resource can have multiple representations. Each of these representations should have similar URIs. In essence, a URI should contain sufficient information needed by the server to produce the desired representation. A representation is actually the description of a resource. The representation of a resource distinctly describes its state information.
    - **Resource link**: This is used to represent another representation of the same resource or another resource.
    - **Resource interface**: This is used to provide an interface to access a resource and manipulate its state information.

Basic concepts of ROAs

The four basic concepts that an ROA implementation should hold include:

- Addressability: Addressability of a resource is its ability to expose its data through well-formed URIs.
- Statelessness: This implies that every HTTP (moreover, because HTTP is a stateless protocol) request occurs in complete isolation.
- Connectedness: Connectedness is the ability of a resource to be connected with another resource. In essence, it is established using links to data of the same kind.
- A uniform interface: A RESTful service should have a uniform interface defined by HTTP's primary methods, that is, GET, PUT, POST, DELETE, and so on. Two or more representations of a particular resource are distinctly identified using URIs.

Fundamental HTTP concepts

In this section, we will discuss the basics of HTTP protocol.

The following table shows the common HTTP methods and their purpose:

Method name	Purpose
`DELETE`	This is used to delete a resource
`GET`	This is used to request for a specific representation of a resource
`HEAD`	This is same as `GET`, but it retrieves only the headers and not the body
`OPTIONS`	This is used to retrieve the methods supported by the resource
`POST`	This is used to post or submit data to be processed by the resource
`PUT`	This is used to create or update data using a particular representation of a resource

The following table shows the HTTP status codes and their purposes:

Status code	Description
100	Informational
200	Successful
201	Created
202	Accepted
300	Redirection
304	Not modified
400	Client error
402	Payment required
404	Not found
405	Method not allowed
500	Server error
501	Not implemented

The following table shows the HTTP redirection status codes:

Status Code	Description
300	Multiple choices
301	Moved permanently
302	Found (temporary redirection)

The following table shows the HTTP error status codes:

Status code	Description
400	Bad request
401	Unauthorized
403	Forbidden
404	Resource not found
405	Method not allowed
408	Request timeout
409	Conflict
413	Request entity too large
415	Unsupported media type

The following table shows the HTTP server error status codes:

Status Code	Description
500	Internal server error
501	Not implemented
503	Service unavailable
505	HTTP version not supported

The following table lists some resource methods and how they can be implemented using the HTTP protocol:

Method name	Description	HTTP operation
`createResource`	This creates a new resource	`PUT`
`getResourceRepresentation`	This is used to retrieve the representation of a particular resource	`GET`
`deleteResource`	This deletes a resource	`DELETE`
`modifyResource`	This modifies a resource	`POST`
`getMetaInformation`	This retrieves metadata of a resource	`HEAD`

In the section that follows, we will explore ROA. We will discuss what a resource implies, the constraints, and so on.

Resource Oriented and Service Oriented Architecture

The SOA and ROA architectural design paradigms provide a way to build robust distributed architectures. In essence, ROA is a specific set of guidelines for a RESTful architecture. ROA is a structural design that provides support for internetworking of resources. A resource is an entity that can be identified using a URI. Servers, computers, computer devices, web pages, scripts, and so on, are all resources in the context of ROA. While SOA is verb oriented, ROA is noun oriented.

ROAs involve retrieval of particular resource instances. Requests in an ROA are stateless. The resource lifecycle management verbs include `PUT`, `DELETE`, `GET`, and `POST`. In an ROA, you have a service provider that maintains a collection of resources. This service provider exposes some basic operations, such as the following:

- Creation of new resources
- Retrieval of resources
- Modification of resources
- Deletion of resources

Here is a list of the core operations supported by RESTful services:

- **GET**: This is an operation that returns the state of the identified resource
- **POST**: This is an operation that is used to update a particular resource
- **PUT**: This operation is used to create a new resource
- **DELETE**: This operation is used to delete or destroy a particular resource

Resource

ROAs mainly thrive on a resource. A resource is a distributed component that is handled using a standard common interface. A resource is essentially defined using a noun. An employee's employment contract is an example of a resource—it describes the data that the resource represents. Note that a resource can be related or linked to other resources. ROA is based on the principle that any entity that can be assigned a uniform resource identifier can be called a resource.

> Note that no two resources can be the same though they can point to the same data. A resource can have one or many URIs. For example, you can have the same sales data available at multiple URIs.

A resource is identified using the following:

- **Resource name**: This is a unique name that identifies a resource
- **Resource representation**: This provides metadata information about the current state of a resource
- **Resource link**: This is a link to the same resource or other resources
- **Resource interface**: This is a uniform interface that is used for assessing the resource and manipulating the state of the resource

Uniform resource identifier

Each resource is identified by having a URI of its own. The URI is the name and address of the resource. URIs should be descriptive, as shown here:

`http://www.packtpub.com/sales/2012/Q4`

`http://www.packtpub.com/sales/2012/Q3`

> Note that a resource can have one or more URIs. For example, the details of the sales figures for Q4 of 2012 can also be available at a different URI, as shown here:
>
> `http://www.packtpub.com/sales/2012/Q4`
>
> `http://www.packtpub.com/sales/year/2012/Q4`
>
> In the preceding example, both the URIs point to the same resource.

Addressability

Addressability is an interesting aspect of every ROA. We may say that an application is addressable if it exposes its data as resources. Now, resources in ROA are exposed using URIs. So, we may say that in order for an application to be addressable, it should expose its data through URIs.

Statelessness

Statelessness is another important aspect of an ROA. This implies that each and every HTTP request is isolated, that is, it occurs in complete isolation.

Representations

Representation is defined as some data that depicts the current state of a resource. For example, when a web server sends data as a series of bytes, it is a representation of a resource.

Comparison of the three architectural styles

When choosing the architectural style that suits your business requirements, there are points aplenty that you have to consider. The following table compares the different architectural styles:

Attribute	Object Oriented	Resource Oriented	Service Oriented
Granularity	Object instances	Resource instances	Service instances
Support for caching responses	No	Yes	No
Payload	Yes, it is usually middleware specific	No, you have nothing that is linked to a particular address or URL	Yes, the WSDL schema
Addressing or request routing	Unique object instance	Unique address of a particular resource	Endpoint address of the service
Coupling between server and client	Tight coupling due to object serialization and early binding to interfaces	Loose coupling due to late binding to resource data	Loose coupling due to late binding to service interfaces

An OOA is best suited when the coupling or cohesion between the server and the client components is tight and is therefore best suited for closed systems.

Service Oriented Architectures involve loose coupling amongst the client and the server components due to late binding to a service interface. These systems are flexible, and tend to scale well because of their stateless nature. These architectures are best suited for shared systems that can work across organization boundaries. The following figure shows the comparison between Service Oriented and Object Oriented architectures:

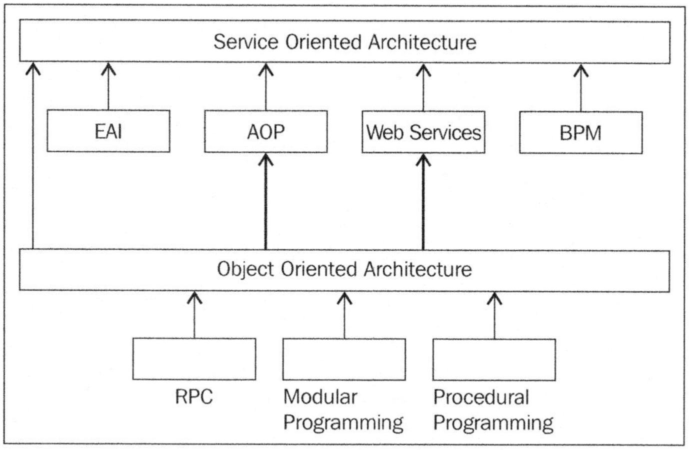

Comparison between SOA and OOA

Resource-oriented systems involve loose coupling between the server and the client components, and they are best suited in scenarios where you need late binding and cache-ability of resource data. These systems are scalable due to their stateless nature.

In essence, ROA is an architectural paradigm that thrives on four basic concepts: resources, the names of the resources, the representations of the resources, and the links between the resources. It is also based on four distinct properties: addressability, statelessness, connectedness, and a uniform interface.

Choosing the right architectural style entirely depends on your business requirements. In essence, you can design a web service application that can use a combination of architectural styles with a resource-oriented approach for simple data reads and a service-oriented approach for complex data operations.

> You can refer to the following site:
>
> `http://www.ics.uci.edu/~fielding/pubs/dissertation/top.htm`

Summary

In OOP, the focus is on creating objects that contain both state and behavior. On the contrary, SOA is built on top of OOP, and allows you to create reusable services. While OOP focuses on what an application comprises, SOA focuses on the functionality of the application. ROA is based on the concept of resources. While a service represents execution of a requested operation, a resource represents the data access mechanism for a particular instance of a given data type. A resource is a distributed component that is handled through a standard, common interface. Resources are addressable using URIs.

This chapter presented a description of the fundamental concepts related to ROA, web services, and SOA. It presented an introduction to ROA and how it differs from other contemporary architectural styles, such as OOP and SOA. We discussed how the three architectural paradigms differ, and also the concepts of ROA.

In the next chapter, we will put all these concepts into practice, discuss the concepts and characteristics of RESTful web services, and explore how we can design and implement RESTful services by using WCF.

3

Working with RESTful Services

Now that we have a good grasp of the concepts of REST and resources, let's explore how we can create RESTful services using WCF. In this chapter, we will discuss WCF in depth, and then create a RESTful service. Note that a RESTful service exposes resources as URIs, and uses HTTP methods to perform CRUD operations.

In this chapter, we will cover the following points:

- Exploring WCF
- WCF bindings
- WCF security
- Creating a WCF service
- Making the WCF service RESTful
- Specifying the binding information
- Hosting the service

We will start this chapter with an in-depth discussion of **Windows Communication Foundation (WCF)** — the technology of choice for building scalable, secure services.

Exploring Windows Communication Foundation (WCF)

Windows Communication Foundation (WCF), is a framework based on the **Service Oriented Architecture (SOA)**. WCF can be used to design applications that can have the ability to intercommunicate. WCF was initially named as "Indigo", and was introduced as part of.NET Framework 3.0 in 2006.

WCF supports unification of the existing .NET technologies. It provides a great platform for unifying Microsoft's distributing technologies—Web Services, Remoting, COM+, and so on, under a single roof. WCF also provides support for cross-platform interoperability, security, service-oriented development, and reliability. It helps you build service-oriented applications by leveraging the benefits of .NET's managed environment.

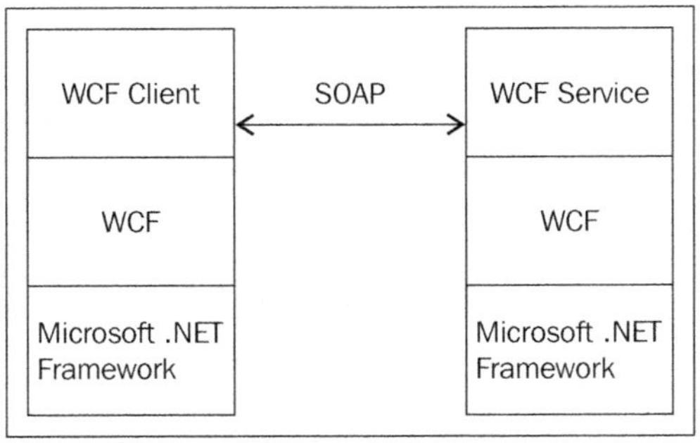

WCF on top of .NET's managed framework

WCF is based on three distinct concepts—address, binding, and contract.

Address implies the location of the service. Binding specifies the communication protocol to be used, that is, it denotes how a particular service can communicate with other services or with other clients. Contract denotes the parts of the service that are exposed. The client connects to the service through the endpoints that are exposed by the service.

Here is the list of the predefined built-in bindings in WCF:

- BasicHttpBinding
- MsmqIntergrationBinding
- WSHttpBinding
- WSDualHttpBinding
- WSFederationHttpBinding
- NetTcpBinding
- NetNamedPipeBinding
- NetMsmqBinding
- NetPeerTcpBinding

Endpoints in WCF are used to associate a service contract with its address. Channel is a bridge between a service and its client. Here are the types of supported channels in WCF:

- Simplex Input
- Simplex Output
- Request-reply
- Duplex

WCF messages can be in one of the following patterns:

- Simplex
- Request-Reply
- Duplex

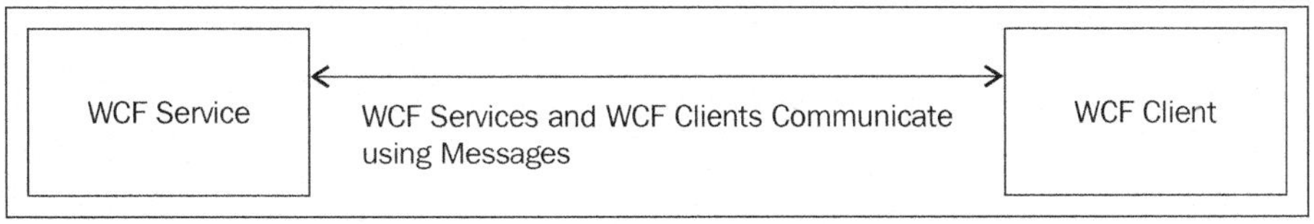

WCF Services and WCF Clients communicate with each other using messages

You can have three contracts in WCF—a service contract, a data contract, and a message contract. Any WCF service class implements at least one service contract—an interface that is used to define the operations that are exposed by the WCF service class. Such operations may also include data operations—exposed using data contracts. A service contract is an interface that is used to define the operations that are exposed by the WCF service class. Actually, a WCF service class is just like any other class, except that it is marked with the ServiceContract attribute. A message contract may be defined as an application that allows you to change the format of the messages. Note that ServiceContract, DataContract, and other related attributes are defined in the `System.ServiceModel` namespace.

Also, any method that is preceded by the OperationContract attribute is externally visible to the clients for SOAP-callable operations. If you have a method that doesn't have this attribute set, the method would not be included in the service contract, and so the WCF client would not be able to access that operation of the WCF service.

Applying service behavior

You can use the ServiceMetadataBehavior attribute element to configure a behavior to apply to a service. This can be done with the following code:

```
<behaviors>
    <behavior>
        <ServiceMetadata httpGetEnabled="true" />
    </behavior>
</behaviors>
<services>
    <service
      name="DemoService"
      <endpoint
         address="http://Joydip-PC:8080/Demo"
         contract="IDemoService"
         binding="basicHttpBinding" />
      </endpoint>
    </service>
</services>
```

New features in WCF 4.5

In this section, we will revisit the new features and enhancements in WCF 4.5. The new and enhanced features in WCF 4.5 include the following:

- **Simplified configuration**: WCF 4.5 provides support for a much simpler configuration. It provides default endpoints, binding, and behavior.
- **Standard endpoints**: WCF 4.5 provides support for preconfigured standard endpoints. The standard endpoints available in WCF 4.5 include dynamicEndPoint, discoveryEndpoint, udpDiscoveryEndpoint, announcementEndpoint, udpAnnouncementEndpoint, mexEndPoint, webHttpEndpoint, webScriptEndpoint, and workflowControlEndpoint.
- **Discovery**: WCF 4.5 provides the ability to resolve service endpoints dynamically, based on some predefined criteria.
- **Simplified IIS Hosting**: WCF 4.5 provides support for simplified hosting services in the IIS with easy-to-use configuration.
- **Better support for REST**: WCF 4.5 provides enhanced support for the design and development of REST-based services.
- **Routing service**: WCF 4.5 provides support for routing. You can host a routing service in much the same way you host a WCF service. Routing service provides versioning, protocol bridging, transaction and error-handling support.

- **Workflow services**: WCF 4.5 provides support for integrating WCF services and WF services. You can now implement declarative services seamlessly. You also have a much improved infrastructure for hosting workflow services in IIS.

Enhancements in the WCF Framework

The WCF Framework was first introduced in 2006 as part of .NET Framework 3.0. It is a framework that comprises a number of technologies to provide a platform for designing applications that are based on SOA, which can have the capability to intercommunicate.

The new enhancements in WCF in .NET Framework 3.5 include the following:

- Support for Ajax-enabled WCF services
- Improved support for WCS standards
- A new WCF designer
- New WCF tools (WcfSvcHost and WcfTestClient)
- Support for REST-based WCF services
- Support for WCF and WF interactivity

Another great new feature in WCF 3.5 is the introduction of the `UserNamePasswordValidator` class. You can use this class to design and implement your own custom validators for validating a user's credentials.

The `UserNamePasswordValidator` class in the `System.IdentityModel.Selectors` namespace can be used to validate user credentials in WCF 3.5. You can create your own custom validator simply by extending the `UserNamePasswordValidator` class and then overriding the Validate method, as shown in the following code:

```
using System;
using System.IdentityModel.Selectors;
using System.IdentityModel.Tokens;
using System.ServiceModel;
namespace Packt
{
    public class PacktValidator : UserNamePasswordValidator
    {
        public override void Validate(String userName, String
            password)
        {
            if (!userName.Equals("joydip")) ||
                !password.Equals("joydip1@3"))
```

```
                {
                    throw new SecurityTokenException("User Name and/or
                        Password incorrect...!");
                }
            }
        }
    }
```

You can then configure the validator you just created in the configuration file, as shown here:

```
<?xml version="1.0" encoding="utf-8" ?>
<configuration>
  <system.web>
    <compilation debug="true" />
  </system.web>
  <system.serviceModel>
    <services>
      <bindings>
        <wsHttpBinding>
          <binding name="PacktAuthentication">
            <security mode="Transport">
              <transport clientCredentialType="Basic" />
            </security>
          </binding>
        </wsHttpBinding>
      </bindings>

      <behaviors>
        <serviceBehaviors>
          <behavior name="PacktValidator.ServiceBehavior">
            <serviceCredentials>
              <userNameAuthentication
                  userNamePasswordValidationMode="Custom"
                  customUserNamePasswordValidatorType=
                  "Packt.PacktValidator, Packt"/>
            </serviceCredentials>
          </behavior>
        </serviceBehaviors>
      </behaviors>
    </system.serviceModel>
</configuration>
```

The new enhancements in WCF 4.5 include the following:

- Simplified configuration
- Standard endpoints

- Discovery
- Simplified IIS Hosting
- REST improvements
- Workflow services
- Routing services
- An automatic Help page

Simplified configuration

WCF 4.5 starts up with the default configuration model. Configuration in WCF 4.5 is much simplified compared to its earlier counterparts. In WCF 3.*x*, you needed to specify the endpoints, behavior, and so on, for the service host. With WCF 4.5, default endpoints, binding information, and behavior are provided by default. In essence, WCF 4.5 eliminates the need for any WCF configuration when you are implementing a particular WCF service.

There are a few standard endpoints and default binding/behavior configurations that are created by default for any WCF service in WCF 4.5. This makes it easy to get started with WCF, because the tedious configuration details of WCF 3.*x* are no longer required.

Consider the following WCF service:

```
using System;
using System.ServiceModel;
namespace PacktService
{
    [ServiceContract]
    public interface ITestService
    {
        [OperationContract]
        String DisplayMessage();
    }

    public class TestService : ITestService
    {
        public String DisplayMessage()
        {
            return "Hello World!";
        }
    }
}
```

In WCF 4.5, you can use `ServiceHost` to host the WCF service without the need for any configuration information whatsoever. The following is all the code you need to host your WCF service and display the address, binding, and contract information:

```
using System.ServiceModel;
using System;
using System.ServiceModel.Description;
namespace PacktClient
{
    class Program
    {
        static void Main(string[] args)
        {
            ServiceHost serviceHost = new ServiceHost
                 (typeof(PacktService.TestService));
                 serviceHost.AddServiceEndpoint
                 (typeof(PacktService.TestService),
                 new BasicHttpBinding(),
                 "http://localhost:1607/
                 TestService.svc");
            serviceHost.Open();
            foreach (ServiceEndpoint serviceEndpoint
                in serviceHost.Description.Endpoints)
              Console.WriteLine("Address: {0}, Binding: {1},
                Contract: {2}", serviceEndpoint.Address,
                serviceEndpoint.Binding.Name,
                serviceEndpoint.Contract.Name);
            Console.ReadLine();
            serviceHost.Close();
        }
    }
}
```

The following is an example of all the configuration information you need to specify and consume your service in WCF 4.5:

```
<?xml version="1.0" encoding="utf-8" ?>
<configuration>
 <system.serviceModel>
    <behaviors>
      <serviceBehaviors>
        <behavior>
          <serviceMetadata httpGetEnabled ="true"/>
        </behavior>
```

```
        </serviceBehaviors>
      </behaviors>
   </system.serviceModel>
  </configuration>
```

Note that the binding used by default is BasicHttpBinding. If you want to choose a more secure binding (such as WSHttpBinding), you can change the binding information, as shown in the following code snippet:

```
<?xml version="1.0" encoding="utf-8" ?>
<configuration>
 <system.serviceModel>
    <behaviors>
      <serviceBehaviors>
        <behavior>
          <serviceMetadata httpGetEnabled ="true"/>
        </behavior>
      </serviceBehaviors>
    </behaviors>
    <protocolMapping>
      <add binding="wsHttpBinding" scheme ="http"/>
    </protocolMapping>
 </system.serviceModel>
</configuration>
```

Standard endpoints

Standard endpoints are preconfigured endpoints in WCF Framework 4.5. You can always reuse them, but they don't generally change. The following table lists the standard endpoints in WCF 4.5 and their purposes.

You can use any of the endpoints shown in the previous example by referencing them in the `<configuration>` element using the endpoint name. The following is an example:

```
<configuration>
  <system.serviceModel>
    <services>
      <service name="PacktService">
        <endpoint kind="basicHttpBinding" contract="IMyService"/>
        <endpoint kind="mexEndpoint" address="mex" />
      </service>
    </services>
  </system.serviceModel>
</configuration>
```

Discovery

There are two modes of operation:

- **Ad-hoc mode**: In this mode, there is no centralized server, and all service announcements and client requests are sent in a multicast manner.
- **Managed mode**: In this mode, you have a centralized server. Such a server is known as a discovery proxy, where the services are published centrally, and the clients who need to consume such published services connect to this mode to retrieve the necessary information.

You can just add the standard `udpDiscoveryEndpoint` endpoint and also enable the `<serviceDiscovery>` behavior to enable service discovery in the Ad-hoc mode. The following is an example:

```
<configuration>
    <system.serviceModel>
      <services>
        <service name="TestService">
          <endpoint binding="wsHttpBinding"
              contract="ITestService" />
          <!-- add a standard UDP discovery endpoint-->
          <endpoint name="udpDiscovery"
              kind="udpDiscoveryEndpoint"/>
        </service>
      </services>
      <behaviors>
        <serviceBehaviors>
        <behavior name="TestService.MyServiceBehavior">
          <!-- To avoid disclosing metadata information, set the
               value below to false and remove the metadata
               endpoint above before deployment -->
          <serviceMetadata httpGetEnabled="true"/>
          <!-- To receive exception details in faults for
              debugging purposes, set the value below to true.
              Set to false before deployment to avoid
              disclosing exception information -->
          <serviceDebug includeExceptionDetailInFaults="false"/>
         <serviceDiscovery />
         </behavior>
      </serviceBehaviors>
      </behaviors>
    </system.serviceModel>
</configuration>
```

In the preceding code snippet, note how a new EndPoint has been added to discover the service. The ServiceDiscovery behavior has also been added. You can use the `DiscoveryClient` class to discover your service and invoke one of its methods.

You must create an instance of the `DiscoveryClient` class and pass `UdpDiscoveryEndPoint` to the constructor of this class as a parameter to discover the service. Once the endpoint has been discovered, its address can be used to invoke the service. The following code snippet illustrates this:

```
using System;
using System.ServiceModel;
using System.ServiceModel.Discovery;
namespace PacktConsoleApplication
{
    class Program
    {
        static void Main(string[] args)
        {
            DiscoveryClient discoverclient = new
                DiscoveryClient(new UdpDiscoveryEndpoint());
            FindResponse findResponse = discoverclient.Find(new
                 FindCriteria(typeof(ITestService)));
            EndpointAddress endpointAddress =
                 findResponse.Endpoints[0].Address;
            MyServiceClient serviceClient = new
                MyServiceClient(new WSHttpBinding(),
                endpointAddress);
            Console.WriteLine(serviceClient.DisplayMessage());
        }
    }
}
```

WCF 4.5 also enables you to configure services to announce their endpoints as soon as they are started. You can configure your service to announce endpoints at start time with the following code:

```
<configuration>
  <system.serviceModel>
    <services>
      <service name="TestService">
        <endpoint binding="wsHttpBinding"
            contract="ITestService"/>
        <endpoint kind="udpDiscoveryEndpoint"/>
      </service>
    </services>
    <behaviors>
```

```
        <serviceBehaviors>
          <behavior>
            <serviceDiscovery>
              <announcementEndpoints>
                <endpoint kind="udpAnnouncementEndpoint"/>
              </announcementEndpoints>
            </serviceDiscovery>
          </behavior>
        </serviceBehaviors>
      </behaviors>
    </system.serviceModel>
</configuration>
```

Simplified IIS hosting

Hosting of WCF 4.5 applications on IIS has now become easy. The following is an example of a simple WCF service:

```
<!-- PacktService.svc -->
<%@ ServiceHost Language="C#" Debug="true" Service=" PacktService
    CodeBehind="~/App_Code/PacktService.cs" %>
[ServiceContract]
public class PacktService
{
    [OperationContract]
    public string GetMessage()
    {
        return "This is a test service.";
    }
}
```

You can then enable service metadata for the service in the application's `web.config` configuration file as shown in the following code snippet:

```
<system.serviceModel>
  <behaviors>
    <serviceBehaviors>
      <behavior>
        <serviceMetadata httpGetEnabled="true"/>
      </behavior>
    </serviceBehaviors>
  </behaviors>
</system.serviceModel>
```

You can also define virtual service activation endpoints for your WCF 4.5 services in your application's `web.config` configuration file. In doing so, you can activate your WCF service without the need of any `.svc` files. Here is the configuration you need to specify in your application's `web.config` configuration file to activate your service without the need of a `.svc` file:

```
<configuration>
  <system.serviceModel>
    <serviceHostingEnvironment>
      <serviceActivations>
        <add relativeAddress="PacktService.svc"
            service="PacktService"/>
      </serviceActivations>
    </serviceHostingEnvironment>
  </system.serviceModel>
</configuration>
```

REST improvements

WCF 4.5 comes with improved support for REST-based features. You now have support for an automatic Help page that describes the REST-based services available for service consumers or clients. This feature is turned on by default, though you can manually configure the same, as shown in the following code listing:

```
<configuration>
  <system.serviceModel>
    <serviceHostingEnvironment aspNetCompatibilityEnabled="true"
      />
    <behaviors>
      <endpointBehaviors>
        <behavior name="PacktTestHelpBehavior">
          <webHttp helpEnabled="true" />
        </behavior>
      </endpointBehaviors>
    </behaviors>
    <services>
      <service name="PacktSampleWCFService">
        <endpoint behaviorConfiguration="PacktTestHelpBehavior"
            binding="webHttpBinding"
            contract="PacktSampleWCFService" />
      </service>
    </services>
  </system.serviceModel>
</configuration>
```

WCF 4.5 also comes with support for HTTP caching using the AspNetCacheProfile attribute. Note that the AspNetCacheProfile support actually uses the standard ASP.NET output caching mechanism to provide you with caching features in your WCF service.

To use this attribute, you should add a reference to the `System.ServiceModel.Web.Caching` namespace. You can apply this attribute in a WebGet operation and specify the cache duration of your choice. The following code snippet can be used in your service contract method to make use of this feature:

```
using System.ServiceModel.Web.Caching;
[OperationContract]
[WebGet]
[AspNetCacheProfile("PacktCache")]
String GetProductName();
```

Accordingly, you should set the cache profile in your application's `web.config` file as shown in the following code:

```
<caching>
 <outputCacheSettings>
    <outputCacheProfiles>
      <add name="PacktCache" duration="60" varyByParam="format"/>
    </outputCacheProfiles>
 </outputCacheSettings>
</caching>
```

Routing service

Routing is a feature in WCF 4.5 that is used to determine how a message should be forwarded, and when a request from the client appears. Filters determine how the routing service redirects the requests that come in from the client to a particular WCF service. These filters are mapped with the corresponding WCF service endpoints using a routing table. The following are the available filter types:

- Action
- Address
- AddressPrefix
- And
- Custom
- Endpoint
- MatchAll
- XPath

The Routing service in WCF 4.5 provides support for the following features:

- Message routing
- Versioning
- Error handling
- Transaction handling
- Protocol bridging

In WCF 4.5, you have the `RoutingService` class that you can use to implement generic WCF routing mechanisms in your application. The following is how the `RoutingService` class looks:

```
[ServiceBehavior(AddressFilterMode = AddressFilterMode.Any,
    InstanceContextMode = InstanceContextMode.PerSession,
    UseSynchronizationContext = false, ValidateMustUnderstand =
    false)]
public sealed class RoutingService : ISimplexDatagramRouter,
    ISimplexSessionRouter,
    IRequestReplyRouter, IDuplexSessionRouter
{
     //Some code
}
```

Hosting RoutingService is as simple as hosting a WCF service. You must simply create an instance of ServiceHost, and then specify RoutingService for the service type. The following is an example:

```
public static void Main()
{
    ServiceHost serviceHost = new
        ServiceHost(typeof(RoutingService));
    try
    {
        serviceHost.Open();
        Console.WriteLine("Routing Service started...");
        Console.WriteLine("Press <ENTER> to stop the Routing
            Service.");
        Console.ReadLine();
        serviceHost.Close();
    }
    catch (CommunicationException ce)
    {
        Console.WriteLine(ce.Message);
        serviceHost.Abort();
    }
}
```

The routing section consists of two sections, filters and filterTables. All the filters that are created for the routing are located in the filters section. For each filter, we have to specify the name and type. Here, the filterData is EndpointName. There are different kinds of filter types available:

- EndpointName
- XPath
- Action
- And
- Custom

Once RoutingService has been started by making a call to the `Open()` method on the ServiceHost instance, it can route messages as needed. The following is an example of a typical configuration you would use to specify the routing information for your routing service:

```
<?xml version="1.0" encoding="utf-8" ?>
<configuration>
 <system.serviceModel>
    <services>
       <service name="System.ServiceModel.Routing.RoutingService"
            behaviorConfiguration="TestBehavior">
        <host>
          <baseAddresses>
            <add baseAddress="http://localhost:1809/TestService"/>
          </baseAddresses>
        </host>
        <endpoint
                  address=""
                  binding="wsHttpBinding"
                  name="TestRoutingEndpoint"
                  contract="System.ServiceModel.Routing.
                  IRequestReplyRouter"/>
      </service>
    </services>
    <behaviors>
      <serviceBehaviors>
        <behavior name="TestBehavior">
          <serviceMetadata httpGetEnabled="True"/>
          <serviceDebug includeExceptionDetailInFaults="True"/>
          <routing routingTableName="ServiceRouterTable"/>
          <!--The Router Table Contains Entries for services-->
        </behavior>
      </serviceBehaviors>
    </behaviors>
```

```
      <!--Define Services Here-->
      <client>
        <endpoint
        name="PacktService" binding="wsHttpBinding"
        address="http://localhost:2709/Services/PacktService.svc"
        contract="*">
        </endpoint>
      </client>
      <!--Routing Defination-->
      <routing>
        <!--Filter For Detecting Messages Headers to redirect-->
        <filters>
          <filter name="TestFilter" filterType="MatchAll"/>
        </filters>
        <!--Define Routing Table, This will Map the service with
            Filter-->
        <routingTables>
          <table name="ServiceRouterTable">
            <entries>
              <add filterName="TestFilter"
                  endpointName="PacktService"/>
            </entries>
          </table>
        </routingTables>
      </routing>
   </system.serviceModel>
  </configuration>
```

Note that the routing service shown in the previous code snippet is hosted at `http://localhost:1809/TestService`. It uses wsHttpBinding.

You can also configure RoutingService with message filters. To do this, you need to enable RoutingBehavior on RoutingService and then specify configuration information, similar to what is shown in the following code snippet:

```
<configuration>
  <system.serviceModel>
    <behaviors>
      <serviceBehaviors>
        <behavior name="PacktServiceRoutingBehavior">
          <serviceMetadata httpGetEnabled="True"/>
          <routing filterTableName="myFilterTable" />
        </behavior>
      </serviceBehaviors>
    </behaviors>
</system.serviceModel>
</configuration>
```

The automatic Help page

The `WebHttpBehavior` class in WCF 4.5 comes with support for an automatic Help page. This class contains a property named `HelpEnabled` that you can turn on or off as needed. Here is how you configure this automatic help feature:

```
<configuration>
  <system.serviceModel>
    <serviceHostingEnvironment aspNetCompatibilityEnabled="true" />
    <behaviors>
      <endpointBehaviors>
        <behavior name="PacktHelpBehavior">
          <webHttp helpEnabled="true" />
        </behavior>
      </endpointBehaviors>
    </behaviors>
    <services>
      <service name="PacktTestService">
        <endpoint behaviorConfiguration="HelpBehavior"
                  binding="webHttpBinding"
                  contract="PacktTestService" />
      </service>
    </services>
  </system.serviceModel>
</configuration>
```

In the next section, we will explore bindings in WCF, and why they are useful.

Bindings in WCF

A binding is used to specify the transport channel (HTTP, TCP, pipes, Message Queuing) and the protocols (Security, Reliability, Transaction flows). A binding comprises of binding elements. These binding elements denote how an endpoint communicates with service consumers. WCF provides support for nine built-in bindings. In WCF, the three major sections in WCF configuration scheme are serviceModel, bindings, and services, shown as follows:

```
<configuration>
    <system.serviceModel>
        <bindings>
        </bindings>
        <services>
        </services>
        <behaviors>
        </behaviors>
    </system.serviceModel>
</configuration>
```

Here's how you specify binding information in the configuration file:

```
<service name="Demo">
  <endpoint
      address="/Test/"
      contract="ITest "
      binding="basicHttpBinding" />
  </endpoint>
</service>
```

The address attribute specifies the URI (absolute or relative path) that other endpoints would use to communicate with the service. The contract attribute denotes the contract that this endpoint is exposing, and the binding attribute is used to select a predefined or custom binding to use with the endpoint. In this section, we will explore bindings in WCF.

BasicHttpBinding

BasicHttpBinding exposes WCF services as legacy ASMX web services, and supports both HTTP and secure HTTP. It supports both Text as well as MTOM encoding methods. However, this type of binding doesn't support `WS-*` standards, such as WS-Addressing, WS-Security, and WS-ReliableMessaging shown as follows:

```
<bindings>
  <basicHttpBinding>
    <binding name="Demo">
      <security mode="Transport">
        <transport clientCredentialType="None"/>
      </security>
    </binding>
  </basicHttpBinding>
</bindings>
```

WsHttpBinding

WsHttpBinding encrypts a SOAP message by default, and supports both HTTP and HTTPS. It supports both Text as well as MTOM encoding methods. It also supports `WS-*` standards, such as WS-Addressing, WS-Security, and WS-ReliableMessaging. This type of binding uses message security by default. You can specify an HTTPS endpoint to provide authentication, integrity, and confidentiality shown as follows:

```
<binding name="Demo">
  <security mode="TransportWithMessageCredential">
    <transport clientCredentialType="None"/>
    <message clientCredentialType="IssuedToken"/>
  </security>
</binding>
```

netTcpBinding

netTcpBinding provides support for transactions and security. It is based on the TCP protocol, and uses binary as the encoding method. It is the most optimized and fastest binding among all the binding types supported by WCF. It uses transport security by default. Note that IIS 6.0 cannot host netTcpBinding applications.

```
<client>
  <endpoint name="Demo" address="net.tcp://localhost:8523/
SecurityService"
    binding="netTcpBinding" contract="ISecurityService" >
    <identity>
      <servicePrincipalName value="SecurityService/Joydip-PC" />
    </identity>
  </endpoint>
</client>
```

MsmqIntegrationBinding

This binding supports transaction, uses transport security, and is optimized for creating WCF clients and services that interoperate with non-WCF MSMQ endpoints. The `MsmqIntegrationBinding` class in the `System.ServiceModel` namespace maps MSMQ messages to WCF messages. MsmqIntegrationBinding provides out of the box binding for communication with MSMQ.

netMsmqBinding

netMsmqBinding uses MSMQ as the transport channel, and is used in a cross machine environment with secure and reliable queued communication. Note that WCF provides support for two bindings to communicate with MSMQ; that is, MsmqIntegrationBinding and netMsmqBinding. Although the former can be used in heterogeneous architectures where WCF is exchanging information with other MSMQ clients and services, the latter is used in homogenous architectures, that is, in architectures where the services and clients are both WCF based.

netNamedPipeBinding

This is typically used for cross-process communication, it uses transport security for message transfer and authentication, supports message encryption and signing, and uses named pipes for message delivery. This binding provides secure and reliable named pipe-based communication between WCF services and WCF clients on the same system. The following code snippet illustrates how a typical service configuration would look when using netNamedPipeBinding:

```
<services>
<service name="DemoService"
    behaviorConfiguration="DemoServiceBehavior">
```

```
        <host>
          <baseAddresses>
            <add baseAddress="net.pipe://localhost/DemoService"/>
          </baseAddresses>
        </host>
    <endpoint address="" binding="netNamedPipeBinding"
        contract="IDemoService"></endpoint>
</service>
</services>
```

And here is how the netNamedPipeBinding client configuration would look like:

```
<client>
<endpoint
    address="net.pipe://localhost/DemoService.svc"
    binding="netNamedPipeBinding"
    contract="IDemoService"></endpoint>
</client>
```

netPeerTcpBinding

This is used to provide secure binding for peer-to-peer network applications. You can use WCF netPeerTCPBinding to develop a peer-to-peer networking applications that make use of a TCP-level peer-to-peer mesh infrastructure. To use this type of binding, you should have **Peer Name Resolution Protocol** (**PNRP**) installed on your machine. If it is not available, you can install it manually using **Add or Remove Programs** in the **Control Panel**. You should also ensure that PNRP and its dependent services are running in your system. The following code snippet illustrates how you can configure netPeerTcpBinding:

```
<endpoint
address="net.p2p://localhost/TestWCFService/"
binding="netPeerTcpBinding"
bindingConfiguration="netp2pBinding"
contract="ITestWCFService">
<bindings>
      <netPeerTcpBinding>
        <binding name="netP2P" >
          <resolver mode="Pnrp" />
          <security mode="None" />
        </binding>
</netPeerTcpBinding>
</bindings>
```

WsDualHttpBinding

WsDualHttpBinding provides all the features of WsHttpBinding. Added to this, it provides support for **Duplex Message Exchange Pattern**. In this pattern, a service can communicate with the client using callbacks. The following code snippet illustrates how you can connect to a WCF service that uses WsDualHttpBinding:

```
Uri serviceAddress = new Uri("http://localhost/DemoService");
WSDualHttpBinding wsd = new WSDualHttpBinding();
EndpointAddress endpointAddress = new
    EndpointAddress(serviceAddress,
    EndpointIdentity.CreateDnsIdentity("localhost"));
client  = new DemoServiceClient (new InstanceContext(this), wsd,
    endpointAddress);
```

The following is the configuration you would specify at the client:

```
<system.serviceModel>
    <bindings>
        <wsDualHttpBinding>
            <binding name="WSDualHttpBinding_IDemoService"
                closeTimeout="00:01:00"
                openTimeout="00:01:00" receiveTimeout="00:10:00"
                sendTimeout="00:00:05"
                bypassProxyOnLocal="false" transactionFlow="false"
                hostNameComparisonMode="StrongWildcard"
                maxBufferPoolSize="524288"
                maxReceivedMessageSize="65536"
                messageEncoding="Text" textEncoding="utf-8"
                useDefaultWebProxy="true">
                <readerQuotas maxDepth="32"
                maxStringContentLength="8192"
                maxArrayLength="16384"
                maxBytesPerRead="4096"
                maxNameTableCharCount="16384" />
                <reliableSession ordered="true"
                    inactivityTimeout="00:10:00" />
                <security mode="Message">
                    <message clientCredentialType="Windows"
                        negotiateServiceCredential="true"
                        algorithmSuite="Default" />
                </security>
            </binding>
        </wsDualHttpBinding>
    </bindings>
    <client>
```

```
        <endpoint address="http://localhost/DemoService/"
            binding="wsDualHttpBinding"
            bindingConfiguration="WSDualHttpBinding_IDemoService"
            contract="IDemoService"
            name="WSDualHttpBinding_IDemoService">
            <identity>
                <dns value="localhost" />
            </identity>
        </endpoint>
    </client>
</system.serviceModel>
```

WsFederationHttpBinding

WsFederationHttpBinding is a type of WS Binding that provides support for federated security. Note that a federated service is one that requires the service consumers to be authenticated using a security token issued by a security token service. The `WSFederationHttpBinding` class and the `wsFederationHttpBinding` element in configuration facilitates exposing a federated service. Note that WSFederationHttpBinding supports message-level security, and you need not select a client credential type when using WSFederationHttpBinding, because the client credential type is always an issued token by default. You can know more on WSFederationHttpBinding at `http://msdn.microsoft.com/en-IN/library/aa347982.aspx`.

Using multiple bindings

You can also have multiple bindings for the same WCF service. The following configuration shows how you can configure a service that uses multiple bindings:

```
<service name="DemoService, Version=2.0.0.0, Culture=neutral,
PublicKeyToken=null">
    <endpoint
        address="http://Joydip-PC:8080/Demo1"
        contract="IDemo, Version=2.0.0.0, Culture=neutral,
          PublicKeyToken=null"
        binding="basicHttpBinding"
        bindingConfiguration="shortTimeout"
    </endpoint>
    <endpoint
        address="http://Joydip-PC:8080/Demo2"
        contract="IDemo, Version=2.0.0.0, Culture=neutral,
          PublicKeyToken=null"
        binding="basicHttpBinding"
        bindingConfiguration="Secure"
     </endpoint>
```

```
</service>
<bindings>
    <basicHttpBinding
        name="shortTimeout"
        timeout="00:00:00:01"
     />
     <basicHttpBinding
        name="Secure" />
        <Security mode="Transport" />
</bindings>
```

You can also achieve the same behavior using the `protocolMapping` section in your configuration file, as follows:

```
<protocolMapping>
    <add scheme="http" binding="basicHttpBinding"
        bindingConfiguration="shortTimeout" />
    <add scheme="https" binding="basicHttpBinding"
        bindingConfiguration="Secure" />
</protocolMapping>
<bindings>
    <basicHttpBinding
        name="shortTimeout"
        timeout="00:00:00:01"
     />
     <basicHttpBinding
        name="Secure" />
        <Security mode="Transport" />
</bindings>
```

The following code snippet shows the endPoints to which a service is listening:

```
ServiceHost host = new ServiceHost(typeof(DemoService), new
Uri("http://localhost:9090/DemoService"));
            host.Open();
Console.WriteLine("Service started...press any key to terminate");
            ServiceEndpointCollection endpoints = host.Description.
Endpoints;
            foreach (ServiceEndpoint endpoint in endpoints)
            {
                Console.WriteLine("The service host is listening at
{0}", endpoint.Address);
            }
            Console.WriteLine("Press any key to terminate the
service.");
            Console.ReadLine();
```

You can also define custom binding by deriving your custom binding class from the `System.ServiceModel.Channels.Binding` class. The following table lists the various bindings in WCF, their transport mode, supported message encoding type, security mode, and their transaction support:

Binding Class	Transport	Message Encoding	Security Mode	Reliable Messaging	Transaction Flow
BasicHttpBinding	HTTP	Text	None	Not Supported	Not Supported
WSHttpBinding	HTTP	Text	Message	Disabled	WS-Atomic Transactions
WSDualHttpBinding	HTTP	Text	Message	Enabled	WS-Atomic Transactions
WSFederationHttp Binding	HTTP	Text	Message	Disabled	WS-Atomic Transactions
NetTcpBinding	TCP	Binary	Transport	Disabled	OleTransactions
NetPeerTcpBinding	P2P	Binary	Transport	Not Supported	Not Supported
NetNamedPipes Binding	Named Pipes	Binary	Transport	Not Supported	OleTransactions
NetMsmqBinding	MSMQ	Binary	Message	Not Supported	Not Supported
MsmqIntegration Binding	MSMQ	Not Supported	Transport	Not Supported	Not Supported

The following table lists the types of bindings in WCF and their supported modes:

Binding Type	Transport mode	Message mode
BasicHttpBinding	Yes	Yes
WSHttpBinding	Yes	Yes
WSDualHttpBinding	No	Yes
NetTcpBinding	Yes	Yes
NetNamedPipeBinding	Yes	No
NetMsmqBinding	Yes	Yes
MsmqIntegrationBinding	Yes	No
wsFederationHttpBinding	No	Yes

Choosing the correct binding

In essence, binding is an attribute of an endpoint, and you can use it to configure transport protocol, encoding and security specifications of a service. Now, which is the binding I should use and when? Here's the rule of thumb:

- **WsHttpBinding**: You can use this type of binding if you need to expose your service over the Internet
- **basicHttpBinding**: You should select this type of binding if you need to expose your WCF service to legacy clients, such as an ASMX Web service
- **NetTcpBinding**: You can go for this type of binding if you need to support WCF clients within an intranet
- **netNamedPipeBinding**: This type of binding is a good choice if you need to support WCF clients on the same machine
- **netMsmqBinding**: You can select this type of binding if you need to support disconnected queued calls
- **wsDualHttpBinding**: You can select this type of binding if you would like to provide support for bidirectional communication between the service and the client

Security in WCF – securing your WCF services

In this section we will discuss how we can secure our WCF services. To secure your WCF service and ensure confidentiality of the data transmitted over the wire, you can bank on the concepts of authentication, authorization, and message or transport security. Although authentication denotes identification of the user's (trying to access the service) credentials, authorization denotes the resources to which an authenticated user can have access. To maintain the integrity of messages, you can digitally sign and encrypt your messages before they are transmitted over the wire.

Transport-level security

Transport-level security provides a point-to-point security between two endpoints, and uses transport protocols, such as TCP, HTTP, and MSMQ. Note that the user credentials passed in this mode of security are protocol dependent. The following figure shows the functioning of transport-level security:

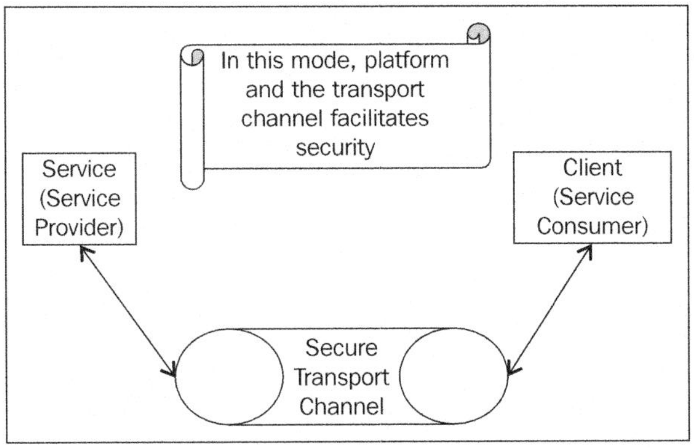

To enable transport security, use the security attribute in the service's configuration file, as shown in the following code snippet:

```
<bindings>
<wsHttpBinding>
<binding name="TransportSecurity">
<security mode="Transport">
<transport clientCredentialType="None"/>
</security>
</binding>
</wsHttpBinding>
</bindings>
```

Message-level security

Message-level security is independent of the security protocol, and here the user credentials are encrypted before they are transmitted over the wire, along with the message. Although transport security works faster than message security, the latter is much more flexible. The following figure shows the functioning of message-level security:

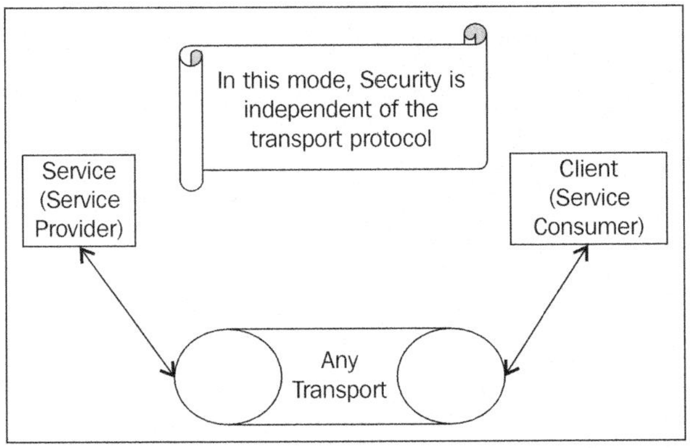

The following code snippet illustrates how you can implement message-level security using user credentials:

```
<wsHttpBinding>
<binding name = "wsHttp">
<security mode = "Message">
<message clientCredentialType = "UserName"/>
</security>
</binding>
</wsHttpBinding>
```

And here is how you can implement the message-level security using certificates:

```
<bindings>
<wsHttpBinding>
<binding name="wsHttpEndpointBinding">
<security>
<message clientCredentialType="Certificate" />
</security>
</binding>
</wsHttpBinding>
</bindings>
```

We have had enough of discussion on WCF (this was needed anyway, because we will be using WCF throughout this book). In the section that follows, we will implement a RESTful service using WCF. We will also create a database that we will be using throughout this book.

Implementing RESTful services using WCF

In this section we will explore how to create REST-based services using WCF. To implement RESTful Web Service, you'll first need to create a WCF service, and then make the service RESTful using the appropriate attributes.

Note that you need to use WebHttpBinding in order to enable the RESTful behavior.

The simplest representation of a WCF RESTful service will look like the following:

```
[AspNetCompatibilityRequirements(RequirementsMode=AspNetCompatibility
RequirementsMode.Required)]
    public class Service : IService
    {
        public Employee[] GetEmployees()
        {
            return new Employee[]
             {
```

```
                    new Employee()
{EmpId=1,FirstName="Joydip",LastName="Kanjilal"},
                    new Employee() {EmpId=2,FirstName="Sabita",LastName
="Kanjilal"}
                };
            }
        }
```

ServiceContract will look like the following:

```
[ServiceContract]
    public interface IService
    {
        [OperationContract]
        [WebGet(UriTemplate="/Employees",ResponseFormat=WebMessageFor
mat.X
  ml )]
        Employee[] GetEmployees();
    }
```

And here is DataContract for you:

```
[DataContract]
    public class Employee
    {
        [DataMember]
        public int EmpId { get; set; }
        [DataMember]
        public string FirstName { get; set; }
        [DataMember]
        public string LastName { get; set; }
    }
```

Creating the security database

In this section, we will create a database to use throughout this book. The name of this database is `Packt_Security`, and it contains the following tables:

- `User`
- `UserAuthentication`
- `UserAuthenticationType`
- `UserLoginHistory`

I've kept the database design as simple as possible. The database design of our `Packt_Security` database looks similar to the following:

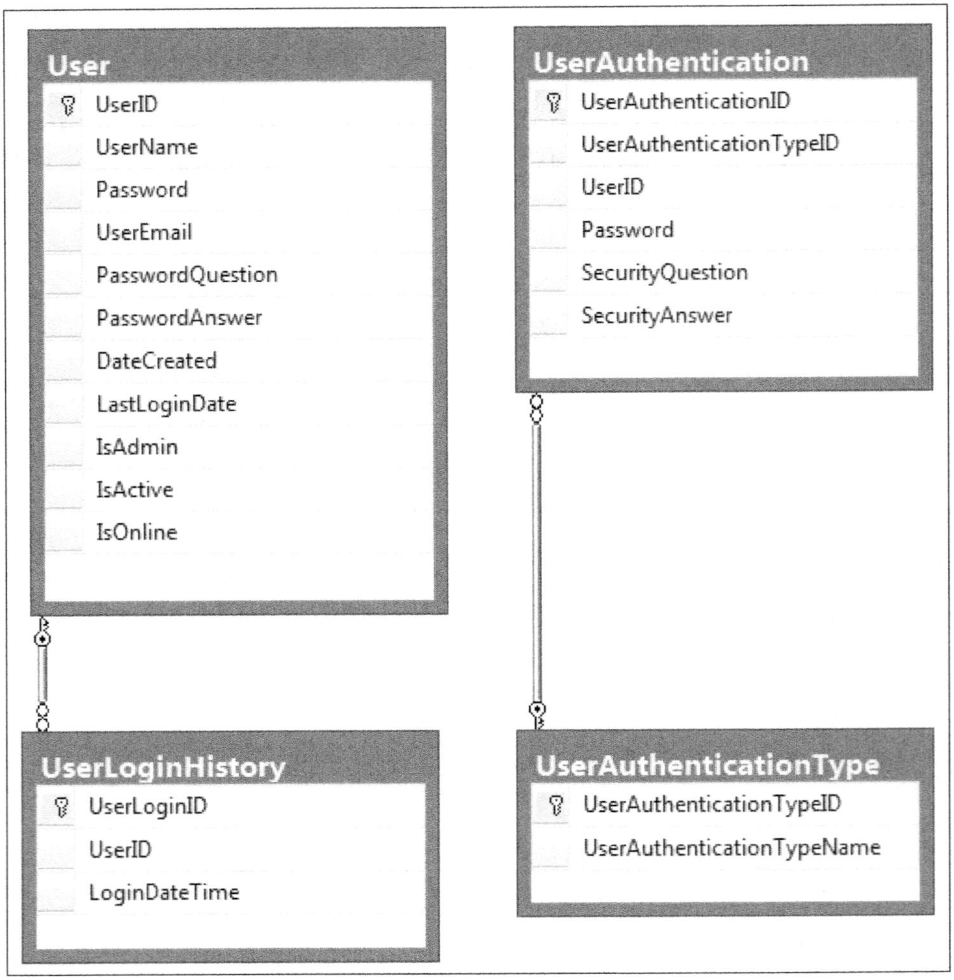

The Database Design

The following is the complete script for the `Security` database:

```
CREATE TABLE [dbo].[UserMaster](
    [UserName] [nvarchar](max) NOT NULL,
    [UserID] [int] IDENTITY(1,1) NOT NULL,
    [UserEmail] [nvarchar](max) NULL,
    [Password] [nvarchar](max) NOT NULL,
    [LastLoginDate] [datetime] NULL,
    [IsOnline] [bit] NULL,
    [IsAdmin] [bit] NULL,
```

```
    [IsActive] [bit] NULL,
    [DateCreated] [datetime] NULL,
 CONSTRAINT [pk_UserMaster] PRIMARY KEY CLUSTERED
(
    [UserID] ASC
)WITH (PAD_INDEX = OFF, STATISTICS_NORECOMPUTE = OFF,
  IGNORE_DUP_KEY = OFF, ALLOW_ROW_LOCKS = ON, ALLOW_PAGE_LOCKS =
  ON) ON [PRIMARY]
) ON [PRIMARY] TEXTIMAGE_ON [PRIMARY]
CREATE TABLE [dbo].[UserLoginHistory](
    [UserLoginID] [int] IDENTITY(1,1) NOT NULL,
    [UserID] [int] NOT NULL,
    [LoginDateTime] [datetime] NOT NULL,
 CONSTRAINT [PK_UserLoginHistory] PRIMARY KEY CLUSTERED
(
    [UserLoginID] ASC
)WITH (PAD_INDEX = OFF, STATISTICS_NORECOMPUTE = OFF,
  IGNORE_DUP_KEY = OFF, ALLOW_ROW_LOCKS = ON, ALLOW_PAGE_LOCKS =
  ON) ON [PRIMARY]
) ON [PRIMARY]
CREATE TABLE [dbo].[UserAuthentication](
    [UserAuthenticationID] [int] IDENTITY(1,1) NOT NULL,
    [UserAuthenticationTypeID] [int] NOT NULL,
    [UserID] [int] NOT NULL,
    [Password] [varchar](50) NOT NULL,
    [SecurityQuestion] [varchar](50) NOT NULL,
    [SecurityAnswer] [varchar](50) NOT NULL,
 CONSTRAINT [PK_UserAuthentication] PRIMARY KEY CLUSTERED
(
    [UserAuthenticationID] ASC
)WITH (PAD_INDEX = OFF, STATISTICS_NORECOMPUTE = OFF, IGNORE_DUP_KEY =
OFF, ALLOW_ROW_LOCKS = ON, ALLOW_PAGE_LOCKS = ON) ON [PRIMARY]
) ON [PRIMARY]
CREATE TABLE [dbo].[UserAuthenticationType](
    [UserAuthenticationTypeID] [int] IDENTITY(1,1) NOT NULL,
    [UserAuthenticationTypeName] [varchar](50) NOT NULL,
 CONSTRAINT [PK_UserAuthenticationType] PRIMARY KEY CLUSTERED
(
    [UserAuthenticationTypeID] ASC
)WITH (PAD_INDEX = OFF, STATISTICS_NORECOMPUTE = OFF, IGNORE_DUP_KEY =
OFF, ALLOW_ROW_LOCKS = ON, ALLOW_PAGE_LOCKS = ON) ON [PRIMARY]
) ON [PRIMARY]
```

We will now implement a WCF service named SecurityService, which will make use of the `UserMaster` table in the Packt database.

Creating SecurityService

To create WCF Service, follow these simple steps:

1. Open Visual Studio 2013 IDE.
2. Go to **File** | **New** | **Project**.
3. Select **WCF Service Application** from the list of the project templates displayed.
4. Specify a name for WCF Service Application.
5. Click on **OK** to save.

Please refer to the following screenshot:

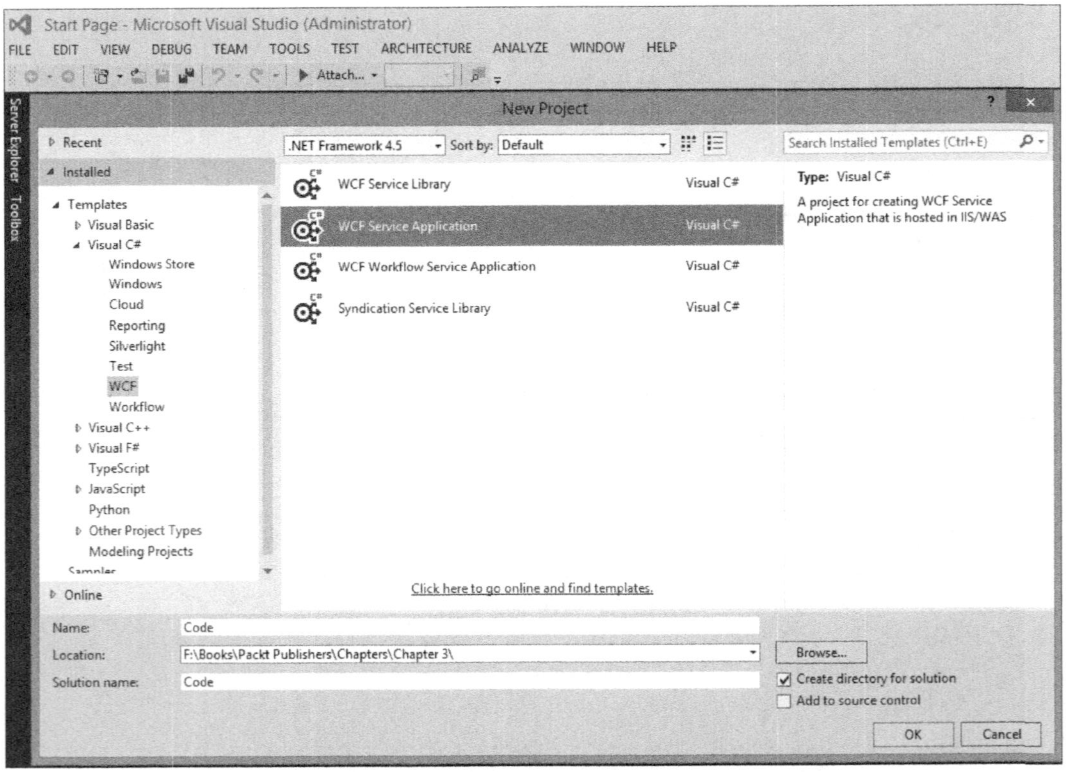

Creating the Service

A WCF service is comprises the following:

- A Service class
- A Service contract
- Hosting environment
- One or more endpoints

A **service class** in WCF is the one that implements a service contract. A **service contract** is typically an interface, and is decorated using the `[ServiceContract]` attribute. The hosting environment denotes the environment in which a WCF service executes. A WCF service can be hosted in IIS, or can be a self-hosted service. Clients connect to a WCF service using the exposed endpoints. In a WCF service, you would have one or more methods that are marked using the `[OperationContract]` attribute.

When you create a new WCF Service Application project, you would see a service contract and a service class created by default. Note that the service contract is marked using the `[ServiceContract]` attribute, shown as follows:

```
using System.Runtime.Serialization;
using System.ServiceModel;
namespace Packt.Services
{
    [ServiceContract]
    public interface IService1
    {
        [OperationContract]
        string GetData(int value);
        [OperationContract]
        CompositeType GetDataUsingDataContract(CompositeType
composite);
    }
    [DataContract]
    public class CompositeType
    {
        bool boolValue = true;
        string stringValue = "Hello ";
        [DataMember]
        public bool BoolValue
        {
            get { return boolValue; }
            set { boolValue = value; }
        }
        [DataMember]
        public string StringValue
        {
            get { return stringValue; }
            set { stringValue = value; }
        }
    }
}
```

The service class implements the service contract defined earlier as follows:

```
using System;
namespace Packt.Services
{
    public class Service1 : IService1
    {
        public string GetData(int value)
        {
            return string.Format("You entered: {0}", value);
        }
        public CompositeType GetDataUsingDataContract(CompositeType
composite)
        {
            if (composite == null)
            {
                throw new ArgumentNullException("composite");
            }
            if (composite.BoolValue)
            {
                composite.StringValue += "Suffix";
            }
            return composite;
        }
    }
}
```

A service contract is an interface that is marked with the `[ServiceContract]` attribute, and contains one or more methods that are exposed using the `[OperationContract]` attribute. The next step is to create your service contract and service class. A service contract can also have one or more Data Contracts. A **Data Contract** is a class that holds data and is marked with the `[DataContract]` attribute.

Making the service RESTful

To make the SecurityService RESTful, you would need to specify the `[WebGet]` or `[WebInvoke]` attributes in your service contract. Although the former indicates that the WCF Service can respond to HTTP Get requests, the latter is used to indicate that the WCF Service can respond to HTTP Post requests. Both belong to the `System.ServiceModel.Web` namespace, and are actually part of the HTTP programming model for WCF.

The following code snippet illustrates how a typical [WebGet] attribute is defined:

```
[WebGet(UriTemplate =
"/sales/getsales.xml",
  BodyStyle = WebMessageBodyStyle.Bare,
  RequestFormat = WebMessageFormat.Xml,
  ResponseFormat = WebMessageFormat.Xml)]
```

The [WebInvoke] attribute can be defined so that your WCF Service can respond to HTTP Post operations:

```
[GetOperationContract]
[WebInvoke(UriTemplate =
"/sales/updatesales.xml?
productcode={code}",
Method = "POST",
BodyStyle = WebMessageBodyStyle.Bare,
RequestFormat = WebMessageFormat.Xml,
ResponseFormat = WebMessageFormat.Xml)]
```

To make the service we created earlier in this article RESTful, just change the contract ISecurityService, and specify the WebGet attribute, as in the following code:

```
[ServiceContract]
    public interface ISecurityService
    {
        [OperationContract]
        [WebGet]
        User GetUserData(Int32 userID);
        [WebInvoke]
        User PostUserData(Int32 userID);
    }
```

To enable the service to run in the ASP.NET compatibility mode, you should decorate your service class with the AspNetCompatibilityRequirements attribute, as shown in the following code:

```
[AspNetCompatibilityRequirements
    (RequirementsMode = AspNetCompatibilityRequirementsMode.Allowed)]
[ServiceBehavior(InstanceContextMode = InstanceContextMode.Single)]
public class PackRESTSerivce : IRestSerivce
{
    //Code implementation goes here
}
```

Hosting Security Service

You would now need to host your service. To do this, you would use the `WebServiceHostfactory` class derived from the `ServiceHost` class. You should choose the `WebServiceHostFactory` class if the service uses WebHttpBinding. If your service uses other types of bindings, you can simply use `ServiceHostFactory` to host the service.

To host Security Service, create a Console application, and add references to the following assemblies:

- System.ServiceModel
- System.ServiceModel.Description
- System.ServiceModel.Web

Next, create an instance of the `WebServiceHostfactory` class, and pass the base address and the service type name as parameters:

```
Uri baseAddress = new Uri("http://localhost/SecurityService");

WebServiceHost host = new WebServiceHost(typeof(SecurityService),
baseAddress);
```

You would now need to specify the service endpoint and service debug behavior for your RESTful service. The following is the complete source code:

```
using System;
using System.ServiceModel.Web;
using System.ServiceModel.Description;
using System.ServiceModel;
using Packt.Services.SecurityService;

namespace Packt.ServiceHost
{
    class Program
    {
        static void Main(string[] args)
        {
            Uri baseAddress = new Uri("http://localhost/
SecurityService");
            using (WebServiceHost host = new WebServiceHost(typeof(Sec
urityService), baseAddress))
            {
                ServiceEndpoint serviceEndpoint = host.AddServiceEnd
point(typeof(ITestService), new WebHttpBinding(), "http://localhost/
PacktServices/SecurityService.svc");
```

```
                ServiceDebugBehavior serviceDebugBehavior = host.
Description.Behaviors.Find<ServiceDebugBehavior>();
                serviceDebugBehavior.HttpHelpPageEnabled = false;
                host.Open();
                Console.WriteLine("The SecurityService is ready...");
                Console.WriteLine("Press enter to terminate...");
                Console.ReadLine();
                host.Close();
            }
        }
    }
}
```

Summary

In this chapter, we explored WCF, WCF bindings, and WCF security. We have also designed our security database and created a RESTful service on top of the database we created. Now that our RESTful service has been created, we will explore how we can consume this service in the next chapter.

4

Consuming RESTful Services

In this chapter, we will discuss how we can consume RESTful Services using various clients to perform CRUD operations.

In this chapter, we will cover the following points:

- Understanding Ajax
- Introducing JSON and jQuery
- An overview of Language Integrated Query (LINQ)
- Consuming Security Service
    - Using an ASP.NET client
    - Using an ASP.NET MVC client
    - Using a WPF client

Before we discuss how we can consume WCF RESTful Services, let's take a quick look at LINQ, because we will be using it for querying data throughout this book.

Understanding AJAX

Asynchronous JavaScript and XML (**AJAX**) is a technology that is used to build applications with fast and responsive user interfaces. AJAX can be used to reduce web page postbacks significantly, thus yielding better response time. Not only can you use AJAX to reduce page hits, but also to submit portions of your web page to the web server in order to reduce network traffic.

> Note that Unobtrusive AJAX is the latest evolution of AJAX. This version of AJAX presents a clean separation of behavior (JavaScript), content (HTML), and presentation (CSS), and can work even when JavaScript is turned off in your browser. Unobtrusive AJAX helps make your web applications work irrespective of whether JavaScript is turned off in your web browser. It works even on a mobile phone, screen reader, or the Web.

The technologies that make up AJAX are as follows:

- **XMLHttpRequest**: The `XMLHttpRequest` object is used for the exchange of data between a server and client. Almost all modern-day browsers have an inbuilt `XMLHttpRequest` object.
- **JavaScript**: This is an interpreted, prototype-based scripting language with support for dynamic typing, which enables the client scripts to interact with the controls in a web browser.
- **DHTML**: This is a collection of technologies that can be used to create interactive, intuitive, and dynamic user interfaces. It is also known as Dynamic HTML.
- **DOM**: **Document Object Model** (**DOM**) is a cross-platform, language-independent standard API, which is used to represent objects in HTML, XHTML, and XML documents.
- **XML**: **Extensible Markup Language** (**XML**) is a flexible text-based markup language, which provides a standard that defines the rules for encoding documents.

The advantages of using AJAX are:

- Improved responsiveness
- AJAX helps us in sending small payloads
- Asynchronous processing and reduced network traffic
- Platform and architecture neutrality

Cross-Origin Resource Sharing (**CORS**) is a concept that enables AJAX requests to be posted to a domain that is different from the domain of the client. The modern-day browsers, such as Internet Explorer 8+, Firefox 3.5+, Safari 4+, and Chrome provide support for CORS. You can get to know more about CORS at `http://www.bennadel.com/blog/2327-Cross-Origin-Resource-Sharing-CORS-AJAX-Requests-Between-jQuery-And-Node-js.htm`.

AJAX is heavily dependent on JavaScript, due to which providing multibrowser support applications that use AJAX is a challenge. Also, usage of AJAX makes your web pages difficult to debug and prone to security threats due to the massive usage of JavaScript.

Introducing JSON and jQuery

JavaScript Object Notation (JSON) is a lightweight text based on an open standard that is used for exchange of data. You can use the JSON data format for serializing and transferring data over the Web. Note that JSON has originated from JavaScript, and is represented using two data structures—ordered lists and name/value pairs. The following definition is provided at `www.json.org`:

> *JSON (JavaScript Object Notation) is a lightweight data-interchange format. It is easy for humans to read and write. It is easy for machines to parse and generate. It is based on a subset of the JavaScript Programming Language, Standard ECMA-262 3rd Edition - December 1999. JSON is a text format that is completely language independent but uses conventions that are familiar to programmers of the C-family of languages, including C, C++, C#, Java, JavaScript, Perl, Python, and many others. These properties make JSON an ideal data-interchange language.*

The following code snippet illustrates how the `toJSONString()` method can be called to convert a string into its equivalent JSON representation:

```
var myObject = new Array();
myObject.push("Joydip Kanjilal");
myObject.push("Prakash Nagar");
myObject.push("Begumpet");
myObject.push("Hyderabad");
myObject.push("500016");
alert(myObject.toJSONString());
```

Note that you will get the desired output from the previous code snippet if your web browser doesn't have native support for JSON.

jQuery is now a mature JavaScript library. It is an open source, cross-browser JavaScript library. You can use jQuery to simplify event handling and animations. It should be noted that jQuery was released in 2006 by John Resig. From then on, this jQuery library has matured a lot, and is now widely popular and acceptable worldwide. jQuery also supports extension points—you can extend this library by attaching a plugin to it. The official jQuery website states the following:

> *jQuery is a fast and concise JavaScript Library that simplifies HTML document traversing, event handling, animating, and AJAX interactions for rapid web development. jQuery is designed to change the way that you write JavaScript.*

The main features of jQuery are as follows:

- **Browser compatibility**: This is a feature that enables the application's user interface to behave the same way in multiple browsers
- **Simplified event handling model**: This is a feature that provides a unified and simplified event handling model based on the DOM elements, with a seamless way to register event handlers on each of the commonly used and implemented browser events

Understanding Language Integrated Query (LINQ)

Language Integrated Query (**LINQ**) is a query translation pipeline that has been introduced as part of the C# 3.0 library. It is a language that is integrated into the language itself. It is an extension of C#, and provides a simplified framework for accessing relational data in a strongly typed and object-oriented way. You can even use LINQ to query data from other data sources—XML, objects, and, collections.

The **Line of Business** (**LOB**) applications are data driven, and they mostly depend on CRUD (Create, Read, Update, and Delete) operations on data. The ORMs are built with this in mind, and provide a simple way to access your database by providing data consistency and data integrity. With some awesome features, such as support for anonymous methods, enumerators and yield, the lambda expression, extension methods, and anonymous types, LINQ is basically a sort of **Domain Specific Language** (**DSL**) for C# or VB.NET. Support for IQueryable, IEnumerable, Func delegates, and the lambda expression in the newer versions of the .NET Framework help in promoting this feature.

LINQ is a part of the new versions of the **C#** and **VB.NET** compilers, and it comes with a powerful set of operators to ease the task of querying different data sources, such as the SQL Server and XML.

A query language is one that is used to query data in our applications. Before LINQ arrived, we used PL-SQL and T-SQL to query data from databases. However, none of these were type safe, and they also didn't have compile-time checks to verify whether the statements were correct at the time of compilation. In LINQ, we have compile-time checks and type safety; hence, your queries will be verified for accuracy at the compile time itself!

LINQ is a new useful feature, available as part of C# 3.0, and allows you to integrate queries right into your programs. It is an extension to the C# language and provides a simplified framework for accessing relational data in a strongly typed and object-oriented manner. Apart from being type safe and the ability to check queries at the time of compilation, you can debug your LINQ queries comfortably—a very important feature indeed. It should be noted that Visual Studio has some limitations for the debugging support of LINQ code. For example, "Edit and continue" is not supported; you are not allowed to step into the predicate code in the debug mode, and the code that gets compiled to the expression tree isn't within the control of the debugger.

LINQ provides support for lazy loading, compiled queries, and extension methods. Extension methods, as the name suggests, are those that enable you to provide extensions to an existing type. These enable you to add new methods to existing types without the need of creating new derived types. An example of an extension method is given as follows:

```
public static class EmployeeExtensions
{
  public IQueryable<T> IsActive<T>(this IQueryable<T> source)
  where T : Employee
  {
    return source.Where(e => (e.JoiningDate < DateTime.Now)
      && (e.LeavingDate == DateTime.Now)
      && e.IsActive == true);
  }
}
```

> There is a way to work around debugging the predicate code though. What you can do is replace the predicate code with a call to a method that contains the predicate code, that is, by creating a wrapper method.

The LINQ library comprises the following important namespaces:

- `System.Linq`: This namespace provides a set of classes and interfaces supporting LINQ queries
- `System.Data.Linq`: This namespace provides a set of classes and interfaces for interacting with the relational database

Data source controls

A data source control acts like a layer in between your data source and the data-bound control. Data bound controls can be any control that actually interacts with the end user while consuming the data services provided by the data source control to which it is bound. It defines certain methods and properties that perform data-specific operations, such as insert, delete, update, and select over the data at the data source while abstracting the data source. Following are the various kinds of DataSource controls that are shipped with the ASP.NET 4.0.

ObjectDataSource

ObjectDataSource control works with in-memory collections. It defines properties, such as `InsertMethod`, `DeleteMethod`, `UpdateMethod`, and `SelectMethod`, which perform basic data storage and retrieval operations. Appropriate methods must be created and mapped to these properties to perform the required task. When one of these properties is used, the ObjectDataSource control actually creates the instance and invokes the appropriate method, and it is destroyed as soon as it completes its execution phase. ObjectDataSource is usually used in the business layer of your application, which assists you to directly bind to the data-bound controls on the presentation layer.

SqlDataSource

The SqlDataSource control allows you to perform standard data operations, such as insert, update, delete, and select on the data persisting in your relation database. The SqlDataSource control is not meant only for the SQL Server database, and can work with any managed ADO.NET provider, which means that you can use the SqlDataSource control with different relational data sources. The SqlDataSource control defines properties, such as `InsertCommand`, `DeleteCommand`, `UpdateCommand`, and `SelectCommand` for performing standard data operations, such as insert, delete, update, and select on the data. The command properties need appropriate queries to be set before using them. When a data control that connects to a SqlDataSource control is updated, the SqlDataSource control creates update parameters for all the columns even though few columns are updated. The control also supports caching capabilities, which assist in improving the performance of the application.

SiteMapDataSource

The SiteMapDataSource control allows you to bind the site map of your website. The site map can represent a hierarchical structure. The SiteMapDataSource control needs an appropriate root node to be specified in a given hierarchy. The SiteMapDataSource control contains properties that allow you to specify the node locations. Primarily, the SiteMapDataSource control is used for the purpose of data navigation, which means you cannot perform standard data operations, such as insert, update, delete, sorting, and paging of the data.

XMLDataSource

The XmlDataSource control is another kind of DataSourceControl. Basically, it represents the data that is in the form of XML. You can access the XML data from the XmlDataSource control by connecting the control to a XML file or XML data embedded as a string within the data source control. Caching in the XmlDataSource control is enabled by default for increasing the performance. You can perform standard data operations, such as insert, delete, update, and select, over the XML data that is represented by the XmlDataSource control. However, operations like sorting and paging are not supported by the XmlDataSource control. The control also provides support for applying XML transformations through an XML stylesheet.

LinqDataSource

LinqDataSource control is a new control that has been introduced in ASP.NET 3.5. It extends DataSourceControl and resides in the `System.Web.UI.WebControls` namespace. It provides a new approach for binding LINQ models to the web controls in your ASP.NET applications. The LinqDataSource control provides properties and events using which you can perform operations such as selecting, filtering, grouping, and ordering of a LINQ data source.

The LinqDataSource data control provides a flexible mechanism to build a data control with a wizard-based workflow. It allows you to perform CRUD operations on the data over a LINQ model with minimal need of writing SQL queries.

The syntax remains the same for whatever data source you use. There is no need to define the queries for the select, delete, update, and insert operations manually.

LINQ provides the concept of a unified data model; all you have to do is focus on your logic, because the LinqDataSource control automatically creates the necessary commands for your needs.

The following example of code shows the syntax of using the LinqDataSource control:

```
<asp:LinqDataSource ID=
  "ldsPurchaseOrderDetails" runat="server" ContextTypeName="
  AdventureWorksDataContext" TableName="PurchaseOrderDetails"
  Select="new (ProductID, UnitPrice, StockedQty)">
</asp:LinqDataSource>
```

In the previous code snippet, `ContextTypeName` refers to the `DataContext` class. Note that a `DataContext` class is created automatically when you create a data model using the LINQ to SQL designer in Visual Studio 2013 IDE. The `TableName` property refers to a collection of the `PurchaseOrderDetail` type. The `Select` property extracts a new anonymous type containing the `ProductID`, `UnitPrice`, and `StockedQty` properties. In conjunction with the previous data source control, data controls such as `DetailsView`, `GridView`, or `ListView` can be used to bind the data. A simple syntax that represents the binding mechanism of a GridView's data source to the LinqDataSource control is as follows:

```
<asp:GridView ID="GridView1" runat="server"
  AutoGenerateColumns="False"
  DataSourceID="ldsPurchaseOrderDetails">
  <Columns>
    <asp:BoundField DataField="ProductID" HeaderText="ProductID"
      ReadOnly="True" SortExpression="ProductID" />
    <asp:BoundField DataField="UnitPrice" HeaderText="UnitPrice"
      ReadOnly="True" SortExpression="UnitPrice" />
    <asp:BoundField DataField="StockedQty" HeaderText="StockedQty"
      ReadOnly="True" SortExpression="StockedQty" />
  </Columns>
</asp:GridView>
```

The following example shows how the LinqDataSource control can be used for binding the in-memory objects to a DropDownList control:

```
<asp:LinqDataSource ID="LinqDataSource1" runat="server"
  ContextTypeName="Packt.Customer"
  TableName="FirstNames"></asp:LinqDataSource>
<asp:DropDownList DataSourceID="LinqDataSource1" runat="server"
  ID="DropDownList1"></asp:DropDownList>
```

In the `Default.aspx.cs` file, we will create a class named `Customer`. The class representation is as as follows:

```
public class Customer
  {
    List<string> names = new List<string>();
    public Customer()
    {
```

```
        names.Add("Joydip");
        names.Add("Sriram");
        names.Add("Sandeep");
        names.Add("Ramesh");
        names.Add("Sandy");
        names.Add("John");
      }
      public List<string> FirstNames { get { return names; } }
    }
```

The following figure illustrates the LINQ architecture:

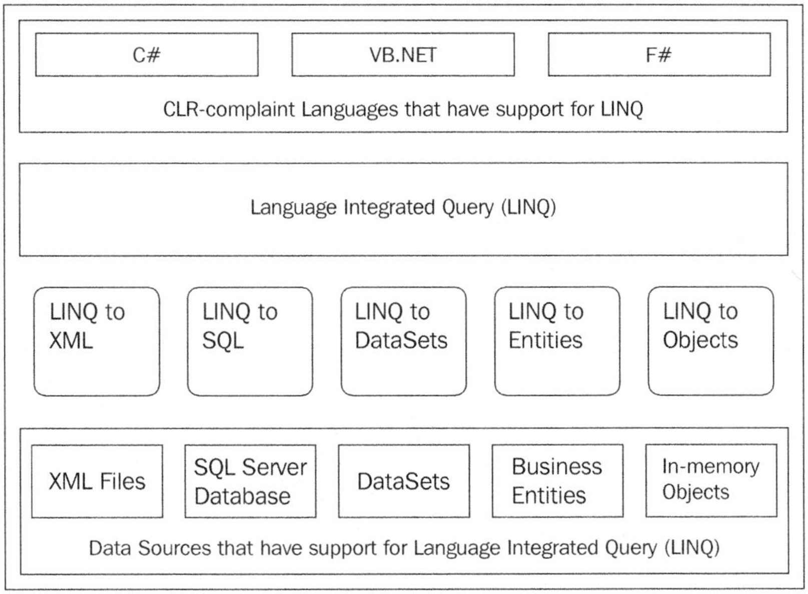

LINQ to XML

"LINQ to XML" maps your LINQ queries or LINQ statements to the corresponding XML data sources. It helps you to use the LINQ standard query operators to retrieve XML data. LINQ to XML is commonly known as XLINQ. You can also use LINQ to query your in-memory collections and business entities (in-memory objects that contain data related to a particular entity) seamlessly.

Support for LINQ to XML is provided in the `System.XML.Linq` namespace. An example that illustrates how LINQ to XML can be used to create a data document is as follows:

```
public static void CreateEmployeeDataSheet()
{
  XDocument doc = new XDocument(
    new XDeclaration("1.0", "utf-8", "yes"),
    new XComment("Employee Data Sheet"),
    new XElement("employees",
    new XElement("Employee",
    new XAttribute("ID", 1),
    new XAttribute("Salaried", "false"),
    new XElement("First Name", "Joydip"),
    new XElement("Last Name", "Kanjilal"),
    new XElement("Joining Date", "02/01/2013")),
    new XElement("Employee",
    new XAttribute("ID", 1),
    new XAttribute("Salaried", "false"),
    new XElement("First Name", "Peter"),
    new XElement("Last Name", "Ward"),
    new XElement("Joining Date", "07/01/2013"))
    )
  );
}
```

LINQ to SQL

Similar to XLINQ (for querying your XML documents), you also have DLINQ which is an implementation of LINQ that allows you to query your databases. LINQ to SQL, or DLINQ as it is called, is actually a very simple ORM tool. It is not a complete ORM tool, because it lacks some of the features that an ORM has. It doesn't support state management and data generation.

> To use LINQ in your programs, you must add a reference to `System.Core.dll` and specify the `System.Linq` namespace in the `using` statement.

LINQ to Objects

LINQ to Objects is another flavor of LINQ that is used to query in-memory collections of objects. Note that LINQ to Objects works with the `T:System.Collections.IEnumerable` or `T:System.Collections.Generic` in-memory objects or a collection of objects. Note that LINQ to Objects is implied as part of LINQ; it is a part of the new versions of the .NET Framework. You need not specify any separate namespaces to write your LINQ to Objects queries.

LINQ to Entities

The ADO.NET Entity Framework is a type of ORM. It is a development platform that provides a layer of abstraction on top of the relational or logical model. In doing so, it isolates the object model of the application from the way the data is actually stored in the relational store. Developers can use the ADO.NET Entity Framework to program against an object model, rather than the logical or relationship model.

This level of abstraction is achieved using the **Entity Data Model (EDM)**—an extended entity relationship model. The EDM reduces the dependency of your domain object model on the database schema of the data store in use. Developers can use the ADO.NET Entity Framework to work with domain-specific properties, such as employee name, employee address, and contact details, without having to be concerned with how the actual data is stored and represented in the underlying data store. The framework can take care of the necessary translations to either retrieve data from your data store or perform insertions, updates, and deletions.

LINQ to Entities is used to query data exposed by the EDM. LINQ to Entities enables you to query your business objects in a strongly typed manner. You can use it to query business objects or collections of business objects from the conceptual data model, that is, the EDM. LINQ to Entities uses ObjectServices to query data from the EDM.

LINQ to Entities uses the Object Services infrastructure to query data from the conceptual model. The `ObjectContext` and `ObjectQuery` classes are two of the most important classes that you use when working with LINQ to Entities. The `ObjectContext` class is used to compose an `ObjectQuery` instance. The generic `ObjectQuery` class actually represents an entity or collection of typed entity instances. It should be noted that LINQ to Entities queries get internally translated to canonical query trees. These, in turn, are converted to corresponding SQL queries internally in a predefined form by your underlying database.

The relation between LINQ to Entities and the Entity Framework is shown in the following figure:

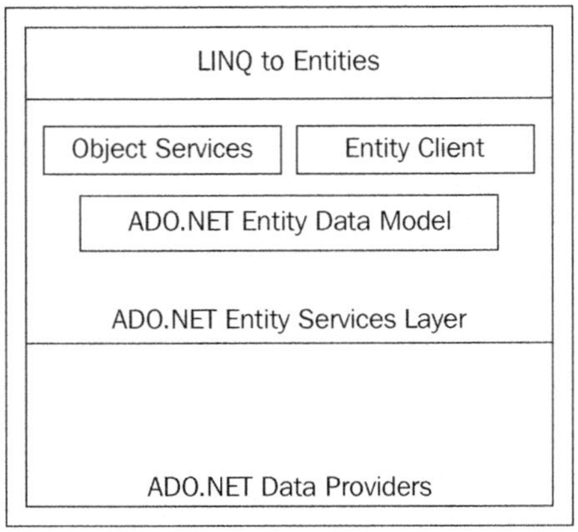

Working with service operations in LINQ

Service operations are the methods that can be called over the data services, which have the same visibility as the entity sets. The `IDataServiceConfiguration` class supports the user-defined methods to be exposed over the data service. To do this, we need to set a `WebGet` attribute to this function and the access rule in the data service configuration of the data service.

The following code snippet illustrates a `DataService` class:

```
[System.ServiceModel.ServiceBehavior(
  IncludeExceptionDetailInFaults = true)]
public class GenericCollections : DataService<AddressSet>
{
  [WebGet]
  public IQueryable<Address> GetAddresssByCity(string City)
  {
    var addressquery = from addr in
      this.CurrentDataSource.Addresses
    where addr.City.Equals(City)
    select addr;
    return addressquery;
  }

  public static void InitializeService(
    IDataServiceConfiguration config)
  {
```

```
        config.UseVerboseErrors = true;
        config.SetEntitySetAccessRule("Addresses",
          EntitySetRights.AllRead);
        config.SetServiceOperationAccessRule("GetAddresssByCity",
          ServiceOperationRights.All);
    }
}
```

Here, we have used `IQueryable<T>` interface so that the method can return an `IQueryable` collection of the type T, where T is a class. The `[WebGet]` attribute allows the method to be accessible in the `HTTP GET` operations. Also, the class attribute `[System.ServiceModel.ServiceBehavior(IncludeExceptionDetailInFaults = true)]` on the GenericCollections class will show the stack trace just in case you encounter any exceptions at the time of execution.

The following code snippet shows how you can query the data exposed by the data service:

```
protected void Page_Load(object sender, EventArgs e)
{
  System.Data.Services.Client.DataServiceContext
    dataServiceContext = new
    DataServiceContext(new
    Uri("http://localhost:2490/GenericCollections.svc"));
  IEnumerable<Address> addresses =
    dataServiceContext.Execute<Address>(new
    Uri("http://localhost:2490/GenericCollections.svc/
    Addresses"));
  var addressquery =
    from address in addresses
    where address.City.StartsWith("S")
    select address;

  foreach (var address in addressquery)
  {
    Response.Write(string.Format("{0}<BR/>{1}<BR/>{2}<BR/><BR/>",
      address.AddressID, address.AddressLine,
      address.City));
  }
}
```

LINQ to SQL allows you to create object models that map to the tables in the relational database. The object-relational mapping implementation of LINQ to SQL handles the execution strategy of the SQL queries. A database markup language file, also known as `.dbml` file, is generated by the Visual Studio IDE when you drag-and-drop database tables from the solution explorer on the LINQ to SQL design surface. When each table is dragged onto the design surface, a class is created for each table. These classes, known as entity classes, are partial classes. They contain a set of partial methods that allow adding custom implementations. The objects to entity classes are known as entities. Associations are automatically created by the LINQ to SQL designer based on the underlying table relationships.

The entity relationships between primary and foreign keys are automatically represented as object relationships by the LINQ to SQL component. The mapping scheme offered by LINQ to SQL provides less housekeeping tasks when tables and columns are changed in the relational database. Only the mapping rules need to be updated without changing the code in your application.

The `AdventureWorksDataContext` class (created using the LINQ to SQL Designer in Visual Studio 2012) looks like the following code:

```
[System.Data.Linq.Mapping.DatabaseAttribute(
  Name="AdventureWorks")]
public partial class AdventureWorksDataContext :
  System.Data.Linq.DataContext
```

> Note that it takes a `DatabaseAttribute` class that specifies the database name. This class also defines several overloaded constructors that can be used for appropriate reasons.

Advantages of LINQ to SQL

The basic advantages of LINQ to SQL over other ORM tools include:

- Developing non-LINQ-to-SQL data-centric applications may consume significant time and effort in trying to build custom components that will interact with the data source. LINQ to SQL maps the tables to classes; this helps architects to design a better n-tier architecture, thus improving the productivity.
- The properties in the entity classes are mapped to the columns in the table with the appropriate data type mapping scheme. Therefore, a compile time check is performed, reducing the runtime errors.
- Another added benefit for the developers is the Intellisense that Visual Studio IDE provides while working with LINQ to SQL applications.

Security Service

Here is the complete code of Security Service that we will use.

The following code snippet illustrates the `ISecurityService` interface. This is the service contract.

```
[ServiceContract]
  public interface ISecurityService
  {
    /// <summary>
    /// GetAllUsers operation contract
    /// </summary>
    /// <returns></returns>
    [OperationContract]
    List<UserAuthentication> GetAllUsers();

    /// <summary>
    /// GetUserByID operation contract
    /// </summary>
    /// <param name="userID"></param>
    /// <returns></returns>
    [OperationContract]
    List<UserAuthentication> GetUserByID(Int32 userID);
  }
```

The following `SecurityService` class implements the `ISecurityService` interface:

```
public class SecurityService : ISecurityService
{
  /// <summary>
  /// GetAllUsers service method
  /// </summary>
  /// <returns>An instance of List<UserAuthentication></returns>
  public List<UserAuthentication> GetAllUsers()
  {
    using (RepositoryBase<SecurityEntities> repository = new
      RepositoryBase<SecurityEntities>("SecurityEntities"))
    {
      return repository.Select<UserAuthentication>().
        ToList<UserAuthentication>();
    }
  }

  /// <summary>
  /// GetUserByID service method
  /// </summary>
  /// <param name="userID">userID as Int32</param>
```

```
    /// <returns>An instance of List<UserAuthentication></returns>
    public List<UserAuthentication> GetUserByID(Int32 userID)
    {
      using (RepositoryBase<SecurityEntities> repository = new
        RepositoryBase<SecurityEntities>("SecurityEntities"))
      {
        return repository.Select<UserAuthentication>().Where( x =>
  x.UserID == userID).ToList<UserAuthentication>();
      }
    }
  }
```

Consuming Security Service

In this section, we will explore how we can consume the `SecurityService` class using ASP.NET and ASP.NET MVC.

ASP.NET

Microsoft's ASP.NET 4.5 is one of the most popular web technologies in recent times. ASP.NET is a web application development framework built on top of **Common Language Runtime** (**CLR**) which you can use to build and deploy web applications and dynamic websites on a managed platform.

Consuming Security Service using ASP.NET 4.5

The following code snippet illustrates how you can consume the `SecurityService` class from an ASP.NET client:

```
  public partial class Default : System.Web.UI.Page
  {
    protected void Page_Load(object sender, EventArgs e)
    {
      if (!IsPostBack)
      {
        BindUserDropDownList();
        BindGrid();
      }
    }

    protected void BindGrid()
    {
      SecurityService serviceObj = new SecurityService();
      var userData = serviceObj.GetAllUsers();
```

```
    if (userData.Count > 0)
    {
      grdUser.DataSource = userData;
      grdUser.DataBind();
    }
  }

  protected void BindGrid(Int32 userId)
  {
    SecurityService serviceObj = new SecurityService();
    var userData = serviceObj.GetUserByID(userId);
    if (userData.Count > 0)
    {
      grdUser.DataSource = userData;
      grdUser.DataBind();
    }

  }
  protected void BindUserDropDownList()
  {
    SecurityService serviceObj = new SecurityService();
    var userData = serviceObj.GetAllUsers();
    if (userData.Count > 0)
    {
      ddlUser.DataSource = userData;
      ddlUser.DataTextField = "UserName";
      ddlUser.DataValueField = "UserID";
      ddlUser.DataBind();
    }

    ListItem li = new ListItem("All", "0");
    ddlUser.Items.Insert(0, li);
  }

  protected void ddlUser_SelectedIndexChanged(object sender,
    EventArgs e)
  {
    if (ddlUser.SelectedValue == "0")
    {
      BindGrid();
    }
    else
    {
      BindGrid(Convert.ToInt32(ddlUser.SelectedValue));
    }
  }
}
```

When you execute the ASP.NET client application, the output looks like the following screenshot:

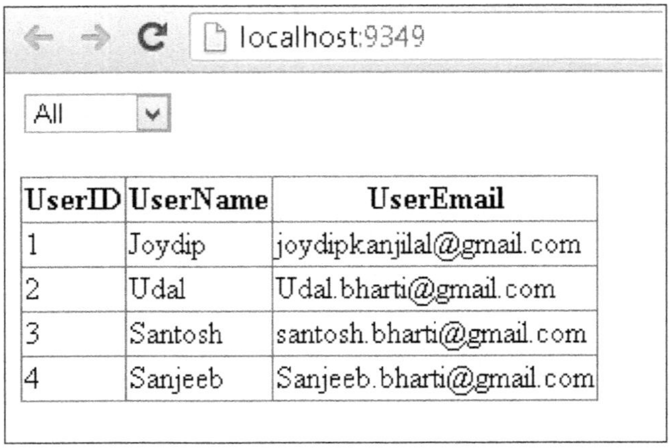

The ASP.NET MVC Framework

The **Model View Controller** (**MVC**) design pattern was invented by Trygve Reenskaug and popularized by the Ruby on Rails framework. Scott Guthrie of Microsoft actually designed the ASP.NET MVC Framework in 2007. The ASP.NET MVC Framework is an application framework based on the popular model view controller design pattern. It helps reduce the cohesion among the components by isolating the concerns in your application.

Usage of the MVC design pattern provides the following benefits:

- Makes your code easier to test, maintain, and deploy
- Facilitates code re-use, maintainability, and testability

The MVC design pattern is comprised of the following major components:

- **The Model**: It is the Data Access layer, and represents the business logic components and the application's data
- **The View**: It is the User Interface or the or the application
- **The Controller**: It is the Business Logic layer and it handles user interactions and updates the model as and when required

The most important benefit of the MVC design pattern is its ability to promote a clean separation of concerns. In doing so, applications that are designed on the MVC pattern are easier to test and maintain.

You can use the MVC design pattern to facilitate code re-use, reduce cohesion among the application's components, and facilitate easier maintenance and testing of the application's components. The ASP.NET MVC Framework is designed based on the MVC Framework, and promises to be the technology of choice for designing web applications in ASP.NET, primarily due to its improved features over the traditional ASP.NET runtime. You can get to know more about the ASP.NET MVC Framework and MVC design pattern from my book titled *ASP.NET 4.0 Programming* by *Mc-Graw Hill Publishing* at `http://www.amazon.com/ASP-NET-4-0-Programming-Joydip-Kanjilal/dp/0071604103`.

Consuming Security Service using ASP.NET MVC

The `HomeController` class extends the controller class of the ASP.NET MVC Framework. It contains a collection of action methods.

We create an instance of the `SecurityService` class in the `HomeController` class. In the `Index()` action method, the `GetAllUsers()` method is called on an instance of `UserAuthenticationModel`. The `userList()` method returns a list of users as a `Json` type.

The following code illustrates the controller class for the ASP.NET MVC client:

```
public class HomeController : Controller
{
  SecurityService serviceObj = new SecurityService();

  public ActionResult Index()
  {
    UserAuthenticationModel userModel = new
      UserAuthenticationModel();
    ViewBag.ListUser = new
      SelectList(serviceObj.GetAllUsers().ToList(), "UserID",
      "UserName");
    return View(userModel);
  }
  private IQueryable<T> SortIQueryable<T>(IQueryable<T> data,
    string fieldName, string sortOrder)
  {
    if (string.IsNullOrWhiteSpace(fieldName)) return data;
    if (string.IsNullOrWhiteSpace(sortOrder)) return data;

    var param = Expression.Parameter(typeof(T), "i");
    Expression conversion =
      Expression.Convert(Expression.Property(param, fieldName),
      typeof(object));
```

```
        var mySortExpression = Expression.Lambda<Func<T,
          object>>(conversion, param);

        return (sortOrder == "desc") ?
          data.OrderByDescending(mySortExpression)
        : data.OrderBy(mySortExpression);
      }

      public JsonResult UserList(string id, string sidx = "UserId",
        string sord = "asc", int page = 1, int rows = 10)
      {
        var userData = serviceObj.GetAllUsers().AsQueryable();
        if (id != null)
        {
          userData = serviceObj.GetUserByID(
            Convert.ToInt32(id)).AsQueryable();
        }
        var sortedDept = SortIQueryable<DataAccess.
          UserAuthentication>(userData, sidx, sord);
        var totalRecords = userData.Count();
        var totalPages = (int)Math.Ceiling((double)totalRecords /
          (double)rows);
        var data = (from s in userData
          select new
        {
          id = s.UserID,
            cell = new object[] { s.UserID, s.UserName, s.UserEmail, }
        }).ToArray();

        var jsonData = new
        {
          total = totalPages,
            page = page,
            records = totalRecords,
            rows = data.Skip((page - 1) * rows).Take(rows)
        };
        return Json(jsonData);
      }
    }
```

When the ASP.NET MVC client application is executed, the output will look like the following screenshot:

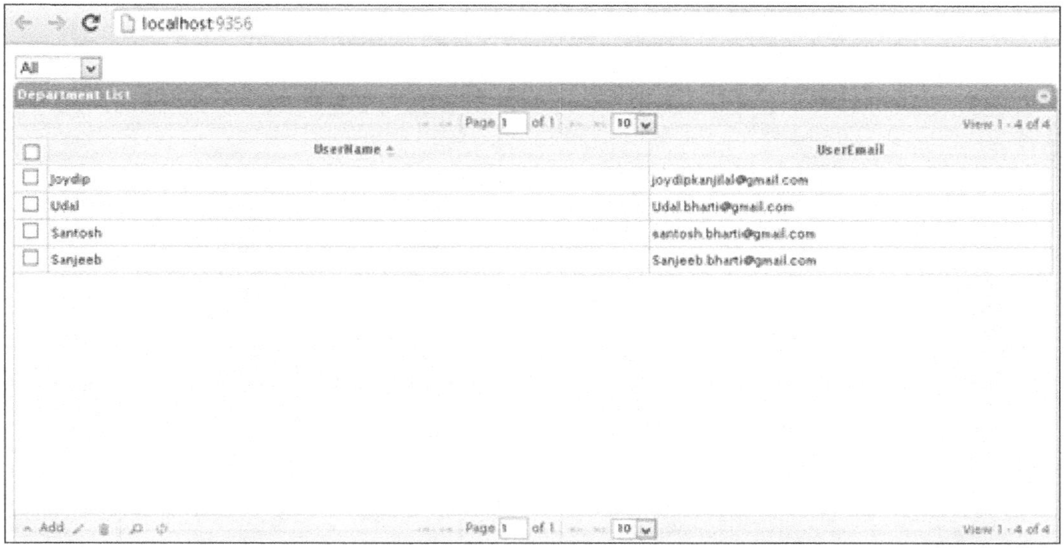

Asynchronous operations

Asynchronous operations help execute operations asynchronously and, hence, leverage the flexibility of the parallel processors of today. Async operations are performed in .NET 4.5 using the `Task` object in .NET Framework 4.5 and MVC 4. The asynchronous programming model of .NET 4.5 is built on top of the existing asynchronous programming model of NET 4.0, and enables you to write methods that return objects of the `Task` type. In essence, the **await** and **async** keywords together with the `Task` object make it easier for you to write asynchronous code in .NET 4.5. This model is also known as **Task-based Asynchronous Pattern (TAP)**. An example of this pattern is as follows:

```
public void Page_Load(object sender, EventArgs e)
{
  RegisterAsyncTask(new PageAsyncTask(LoadData));
}

public async Task LoadSomeData()
{
  var employees = Client.DownloadStringTaskAsync("api/employees");
  var departments = Client.DownloadStringTaskAsync(
    "api/departments");
  var cities = Client.DownloadStringTaskAsync("api/cities");
```

```
    await Task.WhenAll(employees, departments, cities);
    var employeeData = Newtonsoft.Json.JsonConvert.
      DeserializeObject<List<Contact>>(await employees);
    var departmentData = Newtonsoft.Json.JsonConvert.
      DeserializeObject<string>(await departments);
    var cityData = Newtonsoft.Json.JsonConvert.
      DeserializeObject<string>(await cities);
    listEmployees.DataSource = employees;
    listEmployees.DataBind();
}
```

You can also implement asynchronous operations in the ASP.NET MVC Framework using the Async controller. To do this, you should extend your controllers from the abstract `AsyncController` class.

The following code shows how the `AsyncController` class looks:

```
public abstract class AsyncController : Controller,
  IAsyncManagerContainer, IAsyncController, IController
{
  protected AsyncController();
  public AsyncManager AsyncManager { get; }
  protected virtual IAsyncResult BeginExecute(RequestContext
    requestContext, AsyncCallback callback, object state);
  protected virtual IAsyncResult BeginExecuteCore(AsyncCallback
    callback, object state);
  protected override IActionInvoker CreateActionInvoker();
  protected virtual void EndExecute(IAsyncResult asyncResult);
  protected virtual void EndExecuteCore(IAsyncResult asyncResult);
}
```

> Note that the `AsyncManager` class belongs to the `System.Web.Mvc.Async` namespace, and provides the necessary operations for the `AsyncController` class.

You can write your controller by deriving your custom controller class from the `AsyncController` class as shown in the following code:

```
public class HomeController : AsyncController
{
  //Usual code
}
```

The important point to note here is that the name of an asynchronous controller class should have the "Controller" suffix. So, the `Home controller` class can be named `HomeController`, but not "Home" or "ControllerHome". Another interesting point to note here is that you cannot have the sync and async versions of of the same method residing in the same controller.

Therefore, you cannot have both the `Index()` and `IndexAsync()` methods residing in the Index controller class. If you do this, an `AmbiguousMatchException` exception will be thrown.

The following code snippet illustrates a synchronous controller and its action method:

```
public class ProductsController: Controller
{
  public ActionResult GetProducts(int productCode)
  {
    //Usual code
  }
}
```

The following code snippet illustrates an asynchronous controller and its action method:

```
public class ProductsController: AsyncController
{
  public ActionResult GetProducts(int productCode)
  {
    //Usual code
  }
}
```

An async action comprises of a pair of methods that should have the "Async" and "Completed" suffixes, respectively. The following code snippet illustrates this:

```
public class HomeController : AsyncController
{
  public void GetProductsAsync()
  {
    //Some code
  }

  public ActionResult GetProductsCompleted(IList<Product> items)
  {
    //Some code
  }
}
```

> Note that although these APIs are still supported, using the new "async/await" keywords and the `Task` object is a recommended way of implementing asynchronous behavior in your ASP.NET 4.5 applications.

When you define the routes to handle a request asynchronously, you should use the `AsyncMvcRouteHandler` and not the usual `MvcRouteHandler`, as in the following code snippet:

```
routes.Add(new Route("Default.aspx", new AsyncMvcRouteHandler())
{
  Defaults = new RouteValueDictionary(new { controller = "Home",
    action = "Index", id = "" }),
});
```

Understanding Windows Presentation Foundation

Windows Presentation Foundation (WPF), formerly code-named "Avalon," is one of the most widely popular components added to the new versions of the Microsoft .NET Framework for designing and developing windows applications, which can provide visually stunning and rich user interfaces.

The following code snippet illustrates how a typical XAML code for a WPF TextBox control looks:

```
<TextBox SpellCheck.IsEnabled="True" Language="en-US" />
```

The following code snippet can be used to validate the user input and check the spellings based on the locale we specified, that is, `US`.

```
protected override void OnTextInput(TextCompositionEventArgs e)
{
  string data = Text.Remove(SelectionStart,
    SelectionLength) + e.Text;

  if (_regex != null && !_regex.IsMatch(data))
  {
    e.Handled = true;
  }
  else
  {
    base.OnTextInput(e);
  }
}
```

WPF is a graphical subsystem available as part of the latest versions of the .NET Framework. Incidentally, WPF was introduced with the .NET Framework 3.0. WPF enables you to create applications that are rich in UI look and feel, and design applications that are rich in User Interface, media, vector graphics, and so on. XAML provides a declarative touch to WPF. It should be noted that XAML, however, is not specific to WPF or .NET, and the standard is in use by many other technologies.

Consuming Security Service using WPF

The following code illustrates the XAML markup for the WPF client that would consume the `SecurityService` class. I've kept it as simple as possible—with just one Grid control to display user data.

```
<Grid>
  <DataGrid Name="dataGrid1" AutoGenerateColumns="False" >
    <DataGrid.Columns>
      <DataGridTextColumn Binding="{Binding UserID}" Header=
        "User ID" IsReadOnly="True" x:Name="dgrUserID">
      </DataGridTextColumn>
      <DataGridTextColumn Binding="{Binding UserName}"
        Header="User Name" IsReadOnly="True" x:Name="dgrUserName">
      </DataGridTextColumn>
      <DataGridTextColumn Binding="{Binding UserEmail}"
        Header="User Email" IsReadOnly="True"
        x:Name="dgrUserEmail">
      </DataGridTextColumn>

    </DataGrid.Columns>
  </DataGrid>
</Grid>
```

Please refer to the `MainWindow` class given in the following code snippet. The `BindData()` method will be used to bind data to the WPF `DataGrid` class using the SecurityService.

```
public partial class MainWindow : Window
{
  public MainWindow()
  {
    InitializeComponent();
  }

  private void Window_Loaded_1(object sender, RoutedEventArgs e)
  {
```

```
        BindGrid();
    }

    protected void BindGrid()
    {
      SecurityService serviceObj = new SecurityService();
      var userData = serviceObj.GetAllUsers();
      if (userData.Count > 0)
      {
        dataGrid1.ItemsSource = userData.ToList();
      }
    }
}
```

The following figure illustrates how the output of the above program would look:

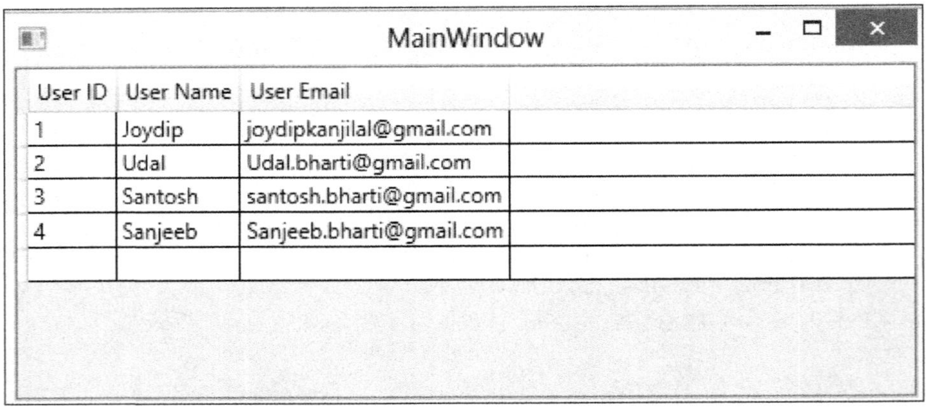

References

- http://www.json.org/
- http://json.codeplex.com/
- http://weblogs.asp.net/scottgu/archive/2007/10/14/aspnet-mvc-framework.aspx

Summary

In this chapter, we explored how we can consume the `SecurityService` class using various clients, that is, theASP.NET, ASP.NET MVC, and WPF clients. In the next chapter, we will explore the new features of ASP.NET 4.5, and also build applications using the ASP.NET Web API.

5

Working with ASP.NET 4.5

In this chapter, we will discuss the new features in ASP.NET 4.5 and explore how we can work with the ASP.NET Web API. The ASP.NET Web API is a lightweight alternative approach like WCF, and uses HTTP as the application protocol.

In this chapter, we will cover the following points:

- Working with the OData protocol
- New features in Microsoft .NET Framework 4.5
- New features and enhancements in ASP.NET 4.5
- Working with the ASP.NET Web API

Working with the OData protocol

The **Open Data protocol** (**OData**) is a protocol that is built on web standards, such as HTTP, Atom, and JSON, and standardizes how the data is exposed and consumed. It is a data access protocol that provides a uniform way of performing CRUD operations on the data. It is used to expose and access information from different data sources; that is, relational databases, filesystems, content management systems, and so on. OData is a standardized protocol that builds on top of core protocols, such as HTTP and architecture paradigms, such as REST. Like RSS, Atom is a way to expose feeds. Note that AtomPub makes use of HTTP verbs such as GET, POST, PUT, and DELETE, to facilitate publishing of data.

Working with the ASP.NET Web API and OData

In this section, we will explore how we can work with the ASP.NET Web API and OData. To install the Web API OData Controller template, right-click on the `Controllers` folder in the solution explorer window, and then select **New Scaffolded Item**. Next, select **Web API 2 OData Controller** with actions using the **Entity Framework**.

To work with the ASP.NET Web API and OData follow these steps:

1. Open the Visual Studio 2013 IDE.
2. Create a new project and save it with a name.
3. In the solution explorer, right-click and select **New Item**.
4. Create an Entity Data Model.
5. Configure the OData route.
6. Implementing the OData controller.

> Note that if you would like to expose an endpoint that adheres to the OData protocol, you should extend your `Controller` class from `ODataController`. On the contrary, if you would like to have a REST endpoint, you should extend your `Controller` class from `ApiController`. Also, you can host multiple OData endpoints vis-a-vis your non-OData endpoints.

The following code snippet illustrates how the `EmployeeController` class would look:

```
public class EmployeeController : ODataController
{
  List<Employee> _employees = DataStore.Employees;

  [Queryable]
  public IQueryable<Employee> GetEmployees()
  {
    return _employees.AsQueryable();
  }

  public Employee GetEmployee([FromODataUri] int employeeID)
  {
     return _employees[employeeID];
  }
}
```

The `[Queryable]` attribute facilitates OData query syntax on a particular action. You can also derive your controller class from `EntitySetController`—a base class for exposing entity sets.

New features in the .NET Framework 4.x

In this section, we will take a look at the striking features in Microsoft .NET Framework 4.*x*.

Supporting asynchronous programming in .NET Framework 4.x

Asynchronous programming is a feature in Microsoft .NET Framework 4.5 that can enhance the overall responsiveness of your application. Support for asynchronous programming is inbuilt in Visual Studio 2012. Asynchronous tasks help write applications that are more responsive and provide a better user experience.

Method calls can either be synchronous or asynchronous. In a synchronous method call, the method is completed in its entirety by the currently executing thread. In an asynchronous method call on the other hand, the currently executing thread begins execution of the method and returns immediately—it doesn't block the user interface in any way. You can execute synchronous threads in Microsoft .NET Framework using the `System.Threading.Thread` namespace. Synchronous threads are those that are executed one after another, that is, in a sequence. In a synchronous operation, two or more threads run in a same context, and therefore the execution of one may block the other.

The support for asynchronous programming is made available through the keywords `async` and `await`. The usage of the keywords `async` and `await` enable you to implement asynchronous programming seamlessly—no callbacks, IAsyncResult, and so on. You can use these two keywords to create asynchronous methods. Note that the asynchronous methods can have three possible return types. These are:

- `Task<TResult>`
- `Task`
- `void`

When `await` keyword is called against that particular task, the method of that task is immediately suspended, and the method resumes its execution once the execution of the task is complete.

Here is a code snippet that illustrates how asynchronous programming can be implemented in Microsoft .NET Framework 4.5:

```
async Task<int> CallWebPagesAsynchronously()
{
    HttpClient client = new HttpClient();
    Task<string> strTask =
      client.GetStringAsync("http://joydipkanjilal.com");
    DoSomeWork();
    string content = await strTask;
    return content.Length;
}
```

Introducing the new features in ASP.NET 4.5

ASP.NET is a server-side technology that runs on top of the managed environment of .NET Framework. You can use ASP.NET to build and deploy web applications and develop dynamic websites. Microsoft .NET Framework is a managed platform used for designing and developing applications that are portable, scalable and robust. Microsoft's ASP.NET stands out as one of the most successful web application development frameworks ever. Over the years, it has matured enough to be the choice of web developers as a framework that you can use to develop highly scalable, high-performance web applications that leverage the features of a managed environment. ASP.NET 4.5 is shipped as part of Visual Studio 2012, and contains many new and interesting features.

Enhanced state management features

ASP.NET 4.5 provides support for improved state management features. The `ViewStateMode` property gives you better control over ViewState. Note that this property can have one of three values: Enabled, Disabled, or Inherit. You have another new property introduced, named `ClientIDMode`. You can use this property to set the ClientID for server controls and use it from the client side. This property can have one of four values: Static, Predictable, Legacy, or Inherit.

The following script code illustrates how you can display the `ClientID` for a control using JavaScript:

```
<script type="text/javascript">
function DisplayClientID()
{
   alert('<%= myButtonControl.ClientID %>');
}
</script>
```

Here's an example that shows how you can use the `ClientIDMode` property:

```
<asp:Panel ID="pnlFirst" runat="server" ClientIDMode="Static">
```

The following code snippet illustrates how the `Predictable` mode is used:

```
<asp:Content ID="contentObj"
  ContentPlaceHolderID="contentPlaceHolderObject" Runat="server">
    <asp:Panel ID="ParentPanel" runat="server"
      ClientIDMode="Static">
        <asp:Panel ID="ChildPanel" runat="server"
          ClientIDMode="Predictable">
            <asp:Button ID="btnSubmit" runat="server"/>
        </asp:Panel>
    </asp:Panel>
</asp:Content>
```

If `ClientIDMode` for a control is set to `Inherit`, the control inherits the `ClientIDMode` setting of its parent control. Here is an example:

```
<asp:Content ID="contentObj"
  ContentPlaceHolderID="contentPlaceHolderObj"
Runat="Server">
    <asp:Panel ID="PanelParent" runat="server">
        <asp:Panel ID="PanelChild" runat="server"
          ClientIDMode="Static">
            <asp:Button ID="btnSubmit" runat="server"
              ClientIDMode="Inherit" />
        </asp:Panel>
    </asp:Panel>
</asp:Content>
```

Performance monitoring

ASP.NET 4.5 enables you to monitor resource utilization. To enable this resource monitoring, all you need to do is to use the following configuration in the `aspnet.config` file:

```
<configuration>
<runtime>
<appDomainResourceMonitoring enabled="true"/>
</runtime>
</configuration>
```

Extensible Output Caching

With ASP.NET 4.*x*, Output Caching has improved a lot. Output Caching is a feature that enables you to store the output of your ASP.NET web pages in cache memory so that subsequent requests to the same web page can be fetched from the memory cache. By doing this, the application's performance can be improved to a great extent for web pages that contain relatively stale data.

With ASP.NET 4.*x*, you have a feature named **Extensible Output Caching** that you can use to add extensibility points to Output Caching. You can now also manage and configure one or more custom Output Cache providers. Here are the Cache Storages for which the ASP.NET 4.*x* Cache API provides support:

- Disk-based Output Caches
- Custom object caches
- Distributed object caches
- Cloud-based object caches

To configure your custom Output Cache provider, all you need to do is to specify the following in the application's `web.config` file:

```
<caching>
<outputCache defaultProvider="Packt.CustomCacheProvider">
<providers>
<add name="DiskCache"
type="Packt.CustomCacheProvider, Packt"/>
</providers>
</outputCache>
</caching>
```

Search Engine Optimization (SEO)

ASP.NET 4.*x* provides support for SEO. The `System.Web.Routing` namespace provides support for routing through the usage of the `RouteTable` and the `PageRouteHandler` classes. You can also achieve SEO using the `Page Meta Keyword` and `Description` features available in ASP.NET 4.5, as given in the following code snippet:

```
protected void Page_Load(object sender, EventArgs e)
{
    this.Page.Title = "Packt";
    this.Page.MetaKeywords = "Books";
    this.Page.MetaDescription = "Packt Books";
}
```

Other notable enhancements

In this section, we will highlight some other notable enhancements in ASP.NET 4.5:

- **Web Sockets**: ASP.NET 4.5 includes full support for the Web Sockets. HTML5 standard is available with ASP.NET 4.5 running on IIS 8.0 via the SignalR library. This allows you to add real-time web functionality to applications easily.
- **Authentication**: With ASP.NET 4.5, you now have a universal provider (`DefaultMembershipProvider`). Also, the OAuth protocol is there. OAuth is an open standard for authorizing clients to enable access to server resources on behalf of a resource owner.
- **Web publishing**: In ASP.NET 4.5, Web publishing feature has been enhanced—you can now compare local and remotes files and publish only the files you need.
- **Web API**: This API is included with ASP.NET 4.5 and its REST-based features for developing and building RESTful applications. Also, the Web API now includes extensive OData support.
- **Leveraging IIS features**: ASP.NET 4.5 enables you to leverage the new features available in **Internet Information Server** (**IIS**) 8.0. These include prefetching and application initialization like an application ping at startup.

Working with the ASP.NET Web API

The ASP.NET Web API is a framework that you can make use of to build web services that use HTTP as the protocol. You can use the ASP.NET Web API to return data based on the data requested by the client; that is, you can return JSON or XML as the format of the data.

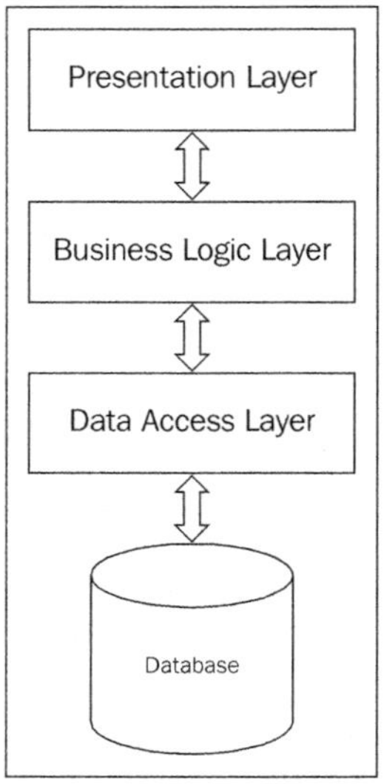

Layers of an application

The ASP.NET Framework runs on top of the managed environment of the .NET Framework.

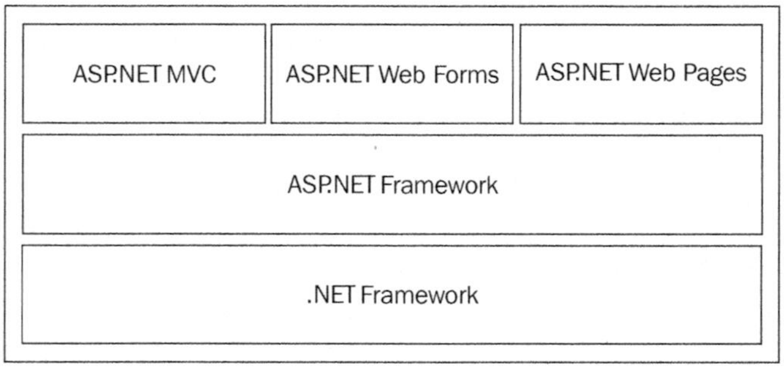

The **Model, View, and Controller** (**MVC**) architectural pattern is used to separate the concerns of an application to facilitate testing, ease the process of maintenance of the application's code, and to provide better support for change. The model represents the application's data and the business objects; the view is the presentation layer component, and the controller binds the Model and the View together. The following figure illustrates the components of Model View architecture:

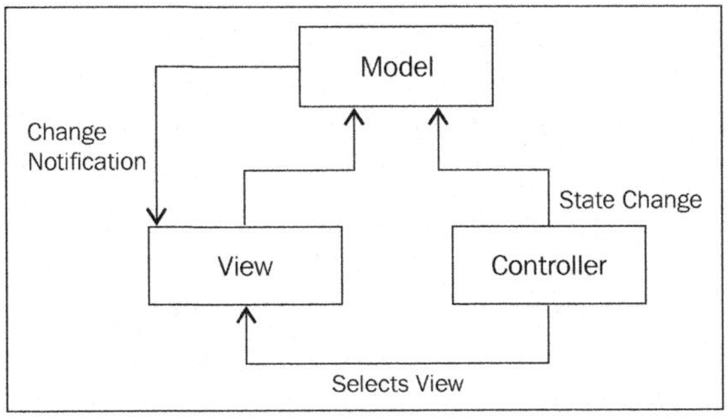

The MVC architecture

The ASP.NET Web API architecture

The ASP.NET Web API is a lightweight web-based architecture that uses HTTP as the application protocol. Routing in the ASP.NET Web API works a bit differently compared to the way it works in ASP.NET MVC. The basic difference between routing in MVC and routing in a Web API is that Web API uses the HTTP method, and not the URI path, to select the action. The Web API Framework uses a routing table to determine which action is to be invoked for a particular request. You need to specify the routing parameters in the `WebApiConfig.cs` file that resides in the `App_Start` directory.

Here's an example that shows how routing is configured:

```
routes.MapHttpRoute(
    name: "Packt API Default",
    routeTemplate: "api/{controller}/{id}",
    defaults: new { id = RouteParameter.Optional }
);
```

The following code snippet illustrates how routing is configured by action names:

```
routes.MapHttpRoute(
    name: "PacktActionApi",
    routeTemplate: "api/{controller}/{action}/{id}",
    defaults: new { id = RouteParameter.Optional }
);
```

The ASP.NET Web API generates structured data such as JSON and XML as responses. It can route the incoming requests to the actions based on HTTP verbs and not only action names. Also, the ASP.NET Web API can be hosted outside of the ASP.NET runtime environment and the IIS Web Server context.

Routing in the ASP.NET Web API

Routing in the ASP.NET Web API is very much the same as in the ASP.NET MVC. The ASP.NET Web API routes URLs to a controller. Then, the control is handed to the action that corresponds to the HTTP verb of the request message. Note that the default route template for an ASP.NET Web API project is `{controller}/{id}`— here the `{id}` parameter is optional. Also, the ASP.NET Web API route templates may optionally include an `{action}` parameter. It should be noted that unlike the ASP.NET MVC, URLs in the ASP.NET Web API cannot contain complex types. It should also be noted that complex types must be present in the HTTP message body, and that there can be one, and only one, complex type in the HTTP message body.

> Note that the ASP.NET MVC and the ASP.NET Web API are two distinctly separate frameworks which adhere to some common architectural patterns.

In the ASP.NET Web API framework, the controller handles all HTTP requests. The controller comprises a collection of action methods—an incoming request to the Web API framework, the request is routed to the appropriate action. Now, the framework uses a routing table to determine the action method to be invoked when a request is received.

Here is an example:

```
routes.MapHttpRoute(
    name: "Packt Web API",
    routeTemplate: "api/{controller}/{id}",
    defaults: new { id = RouteParameter.Optional }
);
```

Refer to the following `UserController` class. Note that it extends the `BaseApiController` class we designed earlier in this chapter:

```
public class UserController <UserAuthentication>: BaseApiController<Us
erAuthentication>
{
    public void GetAllUsers() { }
    public IEnumerable<User> GetUserById(int id) { }
    public HttpResponseMessage DeleteUser(int id){ }
}
```

The following table illustrates the HTTP method and the corresponding URI, Actions, and so on:

HTTP Method	URI	Action	Parameter
GET	api/users	GetAllUsers	None
GET	api/users/1	GetUserByID	1
POST	api/users		
DELETE	api/users/3	DeleteUser	3

The Web API Framework matches the segments in the URI path to the template. The following steps are performed:

1. The URI is matched to a route template.
2. The respective controller is selected.
3. The respective action is selected.

The `IHttpControllerSelector.SelectController` method selects the controller, takes an `HttpRequestMessage` instance, and returns an `HttpControllerDescriptor`. After the controller has been selected, the Web API Framework selects the action by invoking the `IHttpActionSelector.SelectAction` method. This method in turn accepts `HttpControllerContext` and returns `HttpActionDescriptor`. You can also explicitly specify the HTTP method for an action by decorating the action method using the `HttpGet`, `HttpPut`, `HttpPost`, or `HttpDelete` attributes. Here is an example:

```
public class UsersController : ApiController
{
    [HttpGet]
    public User FindUser(id) {}
}
```

You can also use the `AcceptVerbs` attribute to enable HTTP methods other than `GET`, `PUT`, `POST`, and `DELETE`. Here is an example:

```
public class UsersController : ApiController
{
    [AcceptVerbs("GET", "HEAD")]
    public User FindUser(id) { }
}
```

You can also define route by an action name. Here is an example:

```
routes.MapHttpRoute(
    name: "PacktActionApi",
    routeTemplate: "api/{controller}/{action}/{id}",
    defaults: new { id = RouteParameter.Optional }
);
```

You can also override the action name by using the `ActionName` attribute. The following code snippet illustrates two actions: one that supports `GET` and the other that supports `POST`:

```
public class UsersController : ApiController
{
    [HttpGet]
    [ActionName("Token")]
    public HttpResponseMessage GetToken(int userId);

    [HttpPost]
    [ActionName("Token")]
    public void AddNewToken(int userId);
}
```

Implementing the ASP.NET Web API for the Security database

To implement the ASP.NET Web API, you need to create a class that derives from the `ApiController` class. Now, the methods defined in the Web API controller map to the corresponding HTTP methods. You should ensure that the actions you would like to implement in your Web API Controller class is prefixed with the correct request type (`GET`, `POST`, `PUT`, and `DELETE`).

To create an ASP.NET Web API for our `Security` database, follow these steps:

1. Right-click on the solution explorer window.
2. Select **Add New Project**.

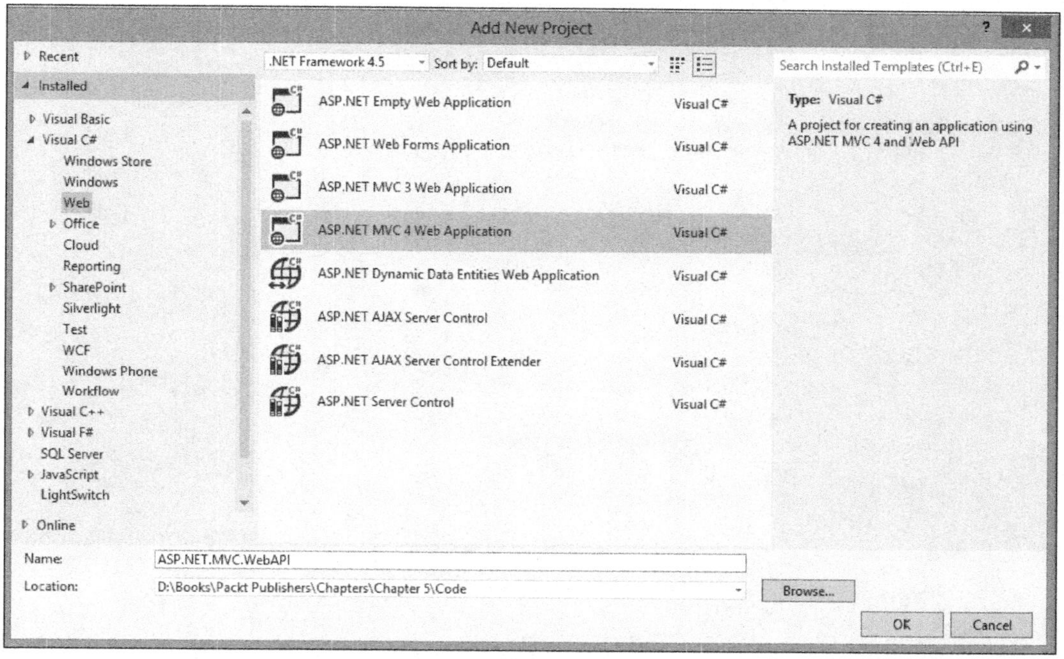

Creating a new ASP.NET Web API project

3. Select **ASP.NET MVC 4 Web Application** from the list of the templates under the **Web** category as shown in the previous figure.
4. Specify a name for the project, and click on **OK**.

5. Select **Web API** as the **Project Template**, as shown in the following screenshot:

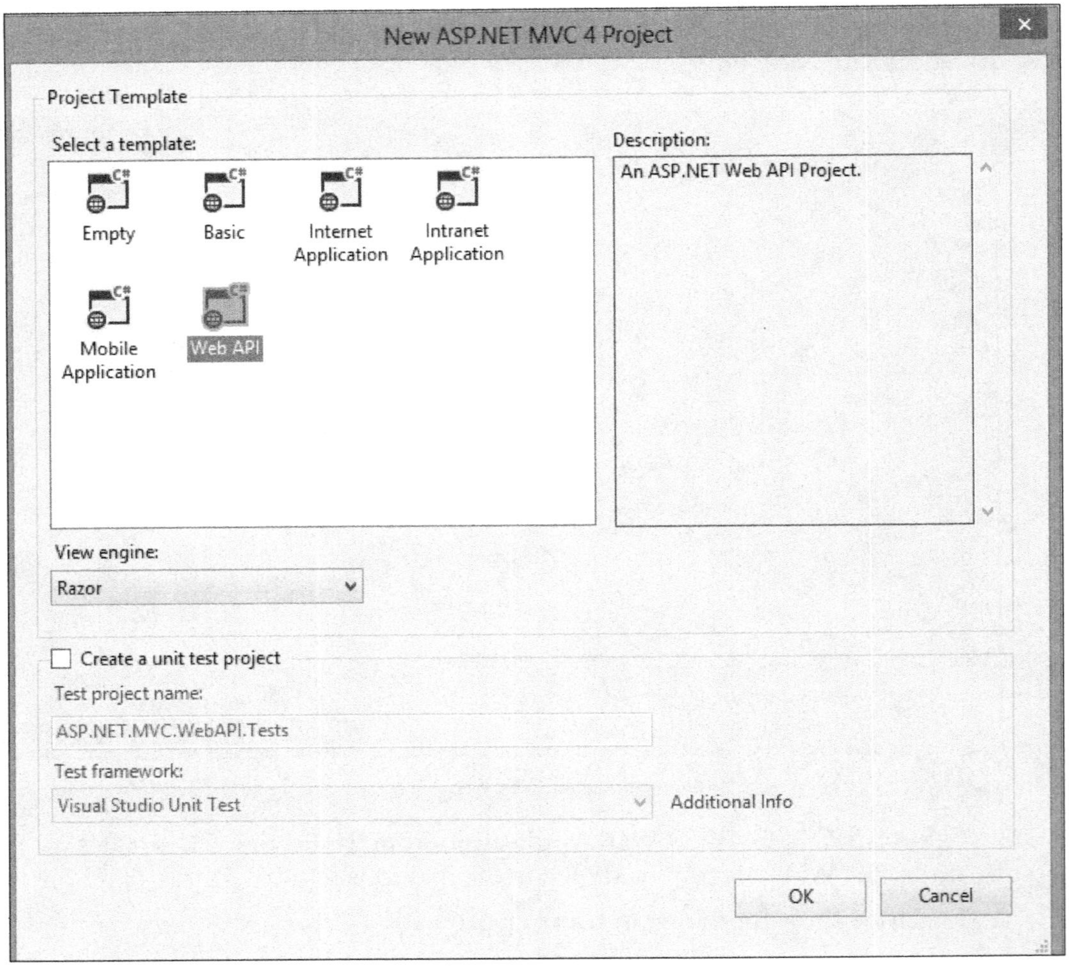

Selecting the project template

6. Ensure that **View engine** selected is **Razor**. Click on **OK** when done.

Here is how the `HomeController` class looks:

```
using System;
using System.Collections.Generic;
using System.Linq;
using System.Web;
using System.Web.Mvc;

namespace ASP.NET.MVC.WebAPI.Controllers
{
```

```
    public class HomeController : Controller
    {
        public ActionResult Index()
        {
            return View();
        }
    }
}
```

Here is how the `ValuesController` class looks:

```
using System;
using System.Collections.Generic;
using System.Linq;
using System.Net;
using System.Net.Http;
using System.Web.Http;
namespace ASP.NET.MVC.WebAPI.Controllers
{
    public class ValuesController : ApiController
    {
        // GET api/values
        public IEnumerable<string> Get()
        {
            return new string[] { "value1", "value2" };
        }

        // GET api/values/5
        public string Get(int id)
        {
            return "value";
        }

        // POST api/values
        public void Post([FromBody]string value)
        {
        }

        // PUT api/values/5
        public void Put(int id, [FromBody]string value)
        {
        }

        // DELETE api/values/5
        public void Delete(int id)
        {
        }
    }
}
```

Now, when you execute the application, here is how the output looks:

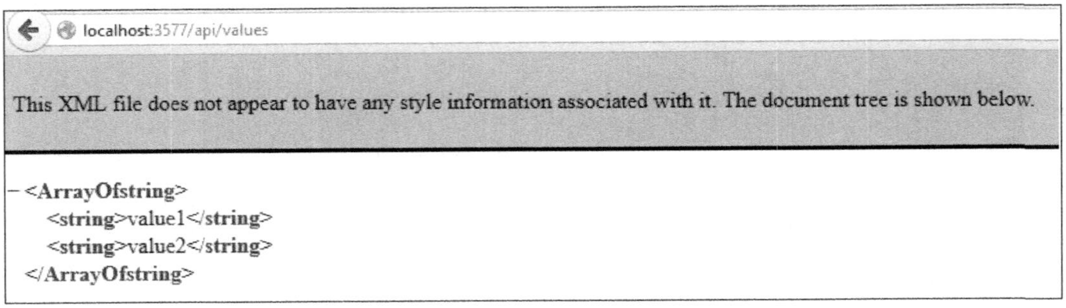

The output in the web browser

Let's create an entity class named `Employee`, and use it in the `ValuesController` class. I've kept the `Employee` class as simple as possible:

```
public class Employee
    {
        public Int32 ID { get; set; }
        public String FirstName { get; set; }
        public String LastName { get; set; }
    }
```

We will now create an array of the `Employee` class and store some data in it using the constructor. Note that an ASP.NET Web API controller derives from `ApiController`. Here is how the updated `ValuesController` class looks:

```
public class ValuesController : ApiController
    {
        Employee[] employeeArray = null;
        public ValuesController()
        {
            employeeArray = new Employee[] {
               new Employee {ID = 1, FirstName = "Joydip",
                 LastName = "Kanjilal"},
               new Employee {ID = 2, FirstName = "Steve", LastName
                 = "Smith"},
               new Employee {ID = 3, FirstName = "Michael",
                 LastName = "Stevens"}
            };
        }
        public IEnumerable<Employee> Get()
        {
            return employeeArray;
        }
```

```
        public string GetFullName(int id)
        {
            return employeeArray[id].FirstName + " " +
              employeeArray[id].LastName;
        }
    }
```

Let's now see how the output looks when we execute the application and invoke the Web API.

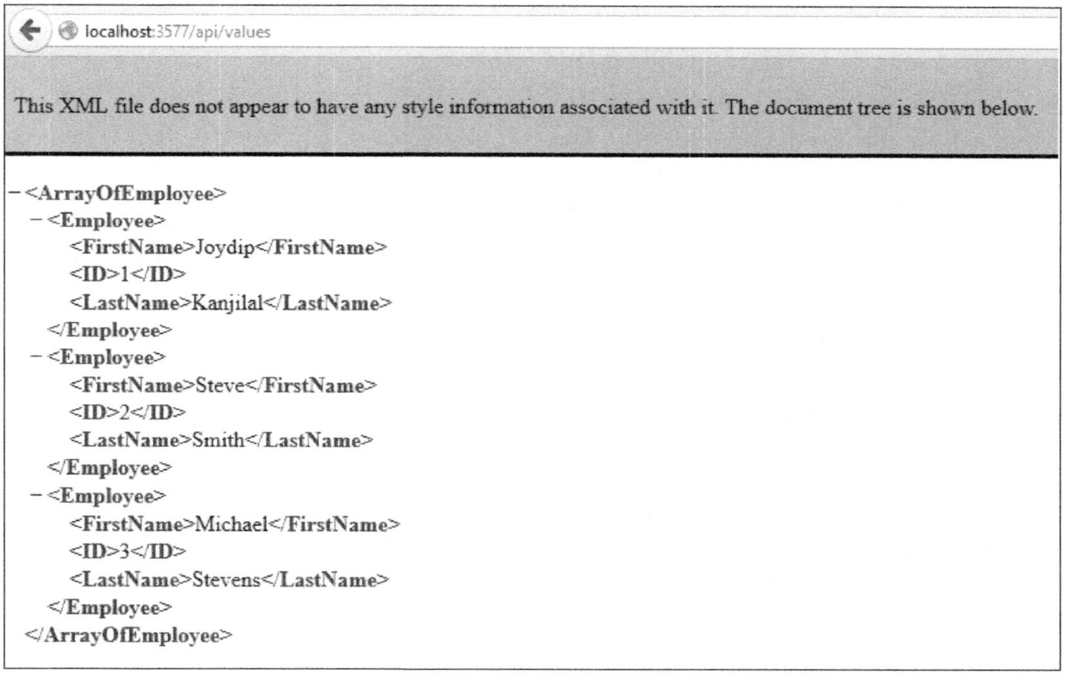

The ValuesController class in execution

Now, let's invoke the Web API controller and pass the Employee ID as the parameter. Here is how the output looks like:

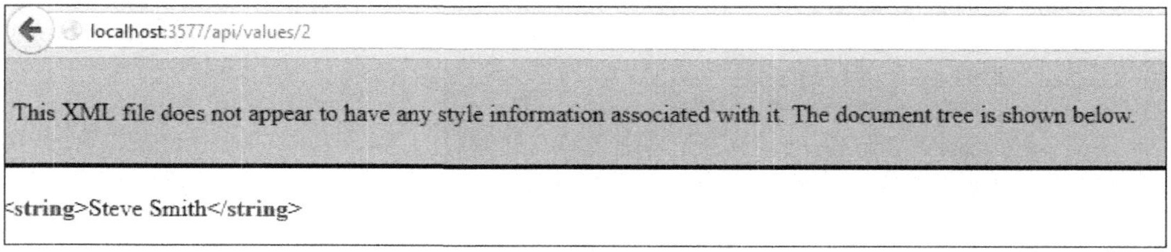

Retrieving a particular record

We will now design a `BaseApiController` class—a class that would serve as base for all controller classes. Here is how the initial version of this class would look:

```
public class BaseApiController<T> : ApiController where T : class
{
    BaseRepository<SecurityEntities> repository = null;
    public BaseApiController()
    {
        repository = new
         BaseRepository<SecurityEntities>
         ("SecurityEntities");
    }
}
```

Here is how the initial version of the `BaseRepository` class looks:

```
public class BaseRepository<TContext> : IDisposable
  where TContext : DbContext, IObjectContextAdapter, new()
{
    private TContext context;

    private BaseRepository()
    {
    }
    public BaseRepository(string connectionStringName)
    {
        context = new TContext();
        context.Database.Connection.ConnectionString =
          "data source=Joydip;initial catalog=SecurityDB;
          integrated security=True;";
    }
}
```

Here's the complete implementation of the `BaseRepository` class:

```
using System;
using System.Linq;
using System.Data.Entity;
using System.Linq.Expressions;
using System.Reflection;
using System.Data.Entity.Infrastructure;
using System.Data;
namespace DataAccess
{
    public class BaseRepository<TContext> : IDisposable
      where TContext : DbContext, IObjectContextAdapter, new()
```

```
    {
        private TContext dataContext;
        private BaseRepository()
        {
        }
        public BaseRepository(string connectionStringName)
        {
            dataContext = new TContext();
            dataContext.Database.Connection.ConnectionString =
              "datasource=Joydip;initial catalog=SecurityDB;
              integrated security=True;";
        }
        public virtual Int32 CreateData<T>(T TObject) where T :
          class
        {
            var dbSetInstance = dataContext.Set<T>().Add(TObject);
            return SaveChanges();
        }
        public virtual Int32 RemoveData<T>(T instance) where T :
          class
        {
            dataContext.Set<T>().Remove(instance);
            return SaveChanges();
        }
        public virtual Int32 EditData<T>(T instance) where T :
          class
        {
            var dbEntityEntry = dataContext.Entry(instance);
            dataContext.Set<T>().Attach(instance);
            dbEntityEntry.State = EntityState.Modified;
            return SaveChanges();
        }
        private Int32 SaveChanges()
        {
            return dataContext.SaveChanges();
        }
        public void Dispose()
        {
            if (dataContext != null)
            {
                dataContext.Dispose();
                dataContext = null;
            }
        }
    }
}
```

Here is how the `IBaseApiController` interface looks:

```
using System;
namespace ASP.NET.MVC.WebAPI.Models
{
    /// <summary>
    /// IBaseApiController interface
    /// </summary>
    public interface IBaseApiController : IDisposable
    {
        int ID { get; set; }
    }
}
```

The `BaseApiController` class extends the `ApiController` class and implements the `IBaseApiController` interface:

```
using System;
using System.Collections.Generic;
using System.Web.Http;
using ASP.NET.MVC.WebAPI.Models;
using DataAccess;
namespace ASP.NET.MVC.WebAPI.Helpers
{
    public class BaseApiController<T> : ApiController where T :
      class, IBaseApiController
    {
        BaseRepository<SecurityEntities> repository = null;
        protected string[] includesArray { get; set; }
        /// <summary>
        /// Default Contructor that initializes the instance of
          BaseRepository
        /// </summary>
        public BaseApiController()
        {
            repository = new BaseRepository
              <SecurityEntities>("SecurityEntities");
        }
        /// <summary>
        /// Get method to retrieve entity data based on the
          generic type supplied
        /// </summary>
        /// <returns></returns>
        public virtual IEnumerable<T> Get()
        {
```

```
            return repository.GetData<T>(includesArray);
        }
        /// <summary>
        /// Get method to retrieve entity data based on the id of
          the entity
        /// </summary>
        /// <param name="id"></param>
        /// <returns></returns>
        public virtual T Get(Int32 id)
        {
            return repository.SearchData<T>(t => t.ID == id,
              includesArray);
        }
        /// <summary>
        /// Post method - edits data
        /// </summary>
        /// <param name="value"></param>
        /// <returns></returns>
        public virtual Int32 Post([FromBody]T value)
        {
            return repository.EditData<T>(value);
        }
        /// <summary>
        /// Put method - creates / inserts new entity
        /// </summary>
        /// <param name="value"></param>
        /// <returns></returns>
        public virtual Int32 Put([FromBody]T value)
        {
            return repository.CreateData<T>(value);
        }
        /// <summary>
        /// Delete method - deletes an existing entity
        /// </summary>
        /// <param name="value"></param>
        /// <returns></returns>
        public virtual Int32 Delete([FromBody]T value)
        {
            return repository.RemoveData<T>(value);
        }
    }
}
```

In a standard ASP.NET MVC project, the route configuration is defined in the `Global.asx.cs` file. On the contrary, in a standard ASP.NET Web API project you would have a `RouteConfig` class and a `WebApiConfig` class inside the `Application_Start` folder.

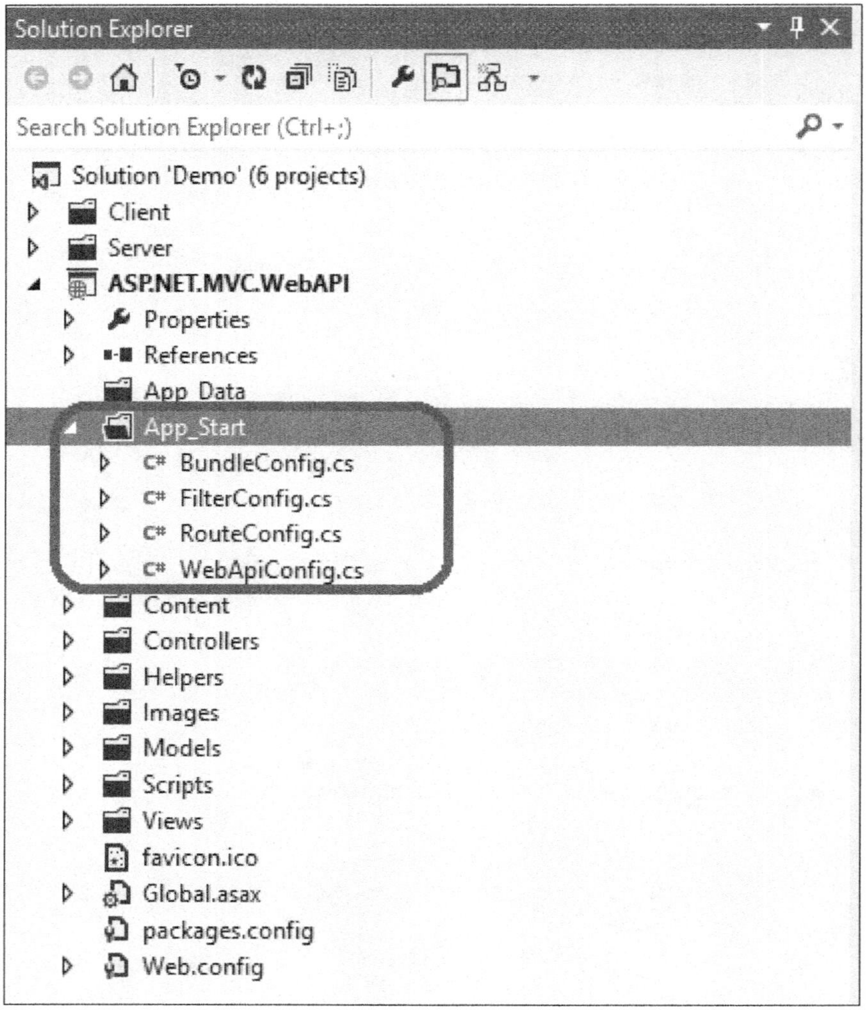

RouteConfig and WebApiConfig in ASP.NET Web API

Note that the `RouteConfig.cs` file is similar to a standard ASP.NET MVC project, and is used to set up routes for the MVC framework. The `WebApiConfig.cs` file is actually where the ASP.NET Web API routing configuration is specified. The `WebApiConfig` class looks like this:

```
using System;
using System.Collections.Generic;
using System.Linq;
uswing System.Web.Http;
namespace ASP.NET.MVC.WebAPI
{
    public static class WebApiConfig
    {
        public static void Register(HttpConfiguration config)
        {
            config.Routes.MapHttpRoute(
                name: "DefaultApi",
                routeTemplate: "api/{controller}/{id}",
                defaults: new { id = RouteParameter.Optional }
            );
        }
    }
}
```

> Here are the links to further references on this topic:
>
> - `http://msdn.microsoft.com/en-us/library/ms171868.aspx`
> - `http://www.asp.net/web-api`
> - `http://idesign.net/articles/asp_net_web_api_vs_wcf.htm`

Summary

In this chapter, we explored the new features in ASP.NET 4.5. We also explored the ASP.NET Web API and implemented an ASP.NET MVC 4 application that uses the ASP.NET Web API framework. We explored the ASP.NET Web API with special focus on how routing and security is handled in the ASP.NET Web API. In the next chapter, we will discuss how we can consume WCF RIA and RESTful Services using Silverlight.

6
Working with RESTful Data Using Silverlight

This is the penultimate chapter of this book in which we will explore how we can consume WCF 4.5 RIA and RESTful services using Silverlight 5.

In this chapter, we will cover the following points:

- Introduction to Silverlight 5
    - New features in Silverlight 5
- Understanding WCF 4.5 RIA Services
- Implementing a sample application that uses WCF 4.5 RIA Services
- Consuming the WCF 4.5 RIA service using a Silverlight 5 client

Introducing Silverlight 5

Silverlight (codenamed Windows Presentation Foundation/Everywhere or WPF/E) is a browser plugin. Silverlight is a client-side technology that provides support for RIA. It can be used to enhance the look and feel of web-based applications. The new versions of Silverlight contain enhanced features for building RIA-based business applications and rich media applications. Cross-browser and cross-platform compatibility and awesome support for rich graphics and animation are some of the striking features of Silverlight. Also, it runs in a sandbox environment—a subset of the WPF Framework.

The newer versions of Silverlight provide great support for Printing (including virtual print preview), COM Automation, Web cam and microphone, **MEF (managed extensibility framework)**, and WCF 4.5 RIA Services. On a different note, the performance of Silverlight 5 applications has been optimized to a great extent.

WCF 4.5 RIA Services provide a framework that helps you to connect .NET client objects with .NET server objects using WCF 4.5. The newer version of Silverlight provides support for WCF 4.5 RIA Services. Note that WCF 4.5 RIA Services (formerly known as .NET RIA services) exposes data in an optimized .NET Binary format or ATOM, JSON, or in an OData format to the Silverlight application. WCF 4.5 RIA Services simplifies the development of RIA applications, that is, applications designed using technologies like Silverlight 5. RIA services provides you with a framework that eliminates the need of duplicating your middle-tier components.

Silverlight provides excellent support for developing the next generation of cross-browser and cross-platform **Rich Internet Applications (RIAs)**. It facilitates the design and development of engaging, interactive user experiences for web and mobile applications. However, Silverlight 5 looks like the last release of Silverlight from Microsoft, and HTML 5 will be the choice going forward.

The choice between opting for Silverlight 5 or HTML 5 depends on many factors. If you are creating a **Line of Business Application (LOB)**, you can choose Silverlight 5 and leverage its data binding features. On the contrary, if you need applications where images, links and textboxes, animations, and interactivity is needed, HTML 5 is a better choice. However, Silverlight 5 is better suited for intranet applications rather than web-based applications. Also, note that Silverlight 5 is only supported on Windows Phones.

New features in Silverlight 5

The following are the new features added to Silverlight 4 and 5:

- Enhancements to controls: The new features added to the controls in Silverlight 5 include: text overflow, support for multi-click, type-ahead text search, incorporation of the `DataContextChanged` event, text tracking, improvements in text rendering, layout, clarity, and so on. In Silverlight 5, you can set the default filename when using the `SaveFileDialog` box using the `DefaultFileName` property. Here is how you can use it:

  ```
  SaveFileDialog fileDialog = new SaveFileDialog();
  fileDialog.DefaultFileName = "Demo.txt";
  fileDialog.ShowDialog();
  ```

- Improvements to data binding.
- XAML changes: In the XAML stack, the features that have been added in Silverlight 5 include: XAML debugging, markup extensions, implicit data templates, binding in styles, and so on. Extensible Application Markup Language or XAML is an XML-based declarative markup language from Microsoft that enables you to design stunning user interfaces for your WPF or Silverlight applications. The XAML content is stored in an `.xaml` file, and you can use XAML to separate the user interface definition of your applications from the runtime logic by using code-behind files.

> Note that XAML debugging works only in Internet Explorer 9 and above.

- Implicit data template is a great new feature that enables you to set a data type using the `DataType` property to the data template, instead of attaching the data template to every control in your page. Here's an example of a code snippet that illustrates this:

```
<ListBox x:Name="users">
<ListBox.ItemTemplate>
<DataTemplate>
<StackPanel>
<TextBlock Text="{Binding FirstName}" FontWeight="Bold" />
<TextBlock Text="{Binding LastName}" />
</StackPanel>
</DataTemplate>
</ListBox.ItemTemplate>
</ListBox>
```

  Mark-up extensions is a feature that enables you to execute code at XAML parsing time . These include `{Binding}`, `{StaticResource}`, `{RelativeSource}`, and so on. You can also create your own custom markup extensions.

- Updates/changes to user interface, graphics, and media.

- Support for Webcam and Microphone: Silverlight 4 and Silverlight 5 enables you to build applications that have the capability of sharing video and audio.
- Optimized performance: Applications built using Silverlight 4 and Silverlight 5 are amazingly fast compared to the earlier versions of Silverlight. Also, Silverlight 5 applications start much quicker. Silverlight 5 provides support for 64-bit operating systems and allows trusted applications to access the local file system without any restriction.
- Enhanced Support for COM Interoperability: Silverlight 4 and Silverlight 5 can interoperate with COM interfaces. The following code snippet shows how to communicate with Microsoft Office applications from Silverlight:

```
dynamic excelObject =
ComAutomationFactory.CreateObject
("Excel.Application");
excelObject.Visible = true;
dynamic workbookObject = excelObject.workbooks;
workbookObject.Add();
dynamic sheetObject = excelObject.ActiveSheet;
```

- To make your Silverlight 4 and Silverlight 5 applications communicate with Microsoft Word, you can write the following piece of code:

```
dynamic wordObject =
ComAutomationFactory.CreateObject
("Word.Application");
wordObject.Documents.Add();
wordObject.Visible = true;
```

- Improved support for RIA services: With Silverlight 5, support for WCF 4.5 RIA Services has been improved. You now have support for complex types, better MVVM support, and also support for much better customization of the generated code.

- Enhanced support for out-of-browser applications: Silverlight 4 and Silverlight 5 provides support for RIA applications, and this support is provided without you having to download and install any additional code or runtime. You now have support for cross-domain network access, accessing user's folders, COM Interop, and HTML hosting.
- Note that you include the following configuration in the `ApplicationManifest.xaml` file, so that you can leverage the elevated permissions while installing and using out-of-browser applications.

```
<OutOfBrowserSettings.SecuritySettings>
<SecuritySettings ElevatedPermissions="Required" />
</OutOfBrowserSettings.SecuritySettings>
```

WCF 4.5 RIA Services

Note that in data centric systems, that is, systems that depend heavily on data, the data can come from disparate systems. Now, your application would need to have the business logic objects and other server objects reside on the client side so that you can access the data.

The major problem with this type of approach is the duplication of code, and also the high consumption of memory resources at the client side. This is where WCF 4.5 RIA Services comes to the rescue. Incidentally, WCF 4.5 RIA Services was introduced in .NET Framework 4 and Silverlight 4. It allows developers to design and implement applications sans the need of a service plumbing code.

The following diagram illustrates the architectural components of a typical WCF 4.5 RIA Services application:

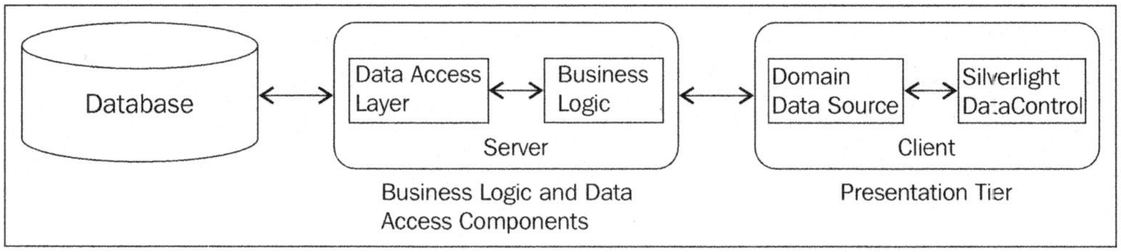

WCF 4.5 RIA Services (built on top of the WCF 4.5 services) simplifies n-tier application development (especially applications that use Silverlight) without you having to write a service plumbing code. In essence, if you use WCF 4.5 RIA Services, your application logic can reside on the server. This can be made available to the client without the need of duplication of the application's logic components on the client side, that is, at the service consumer's end. RIA services are built on top of WCF 4.5, and simplify the client-side programming model. However, there are a few potential drawbacks of RIA services too. Most importantly, working with metadata is a pain, especially when you need to update your model often. If you have a database that contains many entities, you would end up spending more time updating your model when you are using RIA services.

> If you use WCF 4.5 RIA Services, the service consumer can get the latest updates as soon as your business logic components at the server side changes.

Here is a quick look at the features provided by WCF 4.5 RIA Services:

- When you use WCF 4.5 RIA Services, the client-side instances are created through a reflection depending on the server-side objects, in lieu of service contracts, that are exposed by the services that execute on the server.
- WCF 4.5 RIA Services provide support for serializing LINQ queries; so, you can write your LINQ queries at the client side and execute it at the server end.

Implementing a sample application

In this section, we will implement a sample application that illustrates how you can design and implement a WCF 4.5 RIA Service and then consume it using Silverlight 5. When you create a Silverlight application, you can check the **Enable WCF RIA Services** checkbox. This will ensure that an RIA services link is created, when you eventually build the complete solution, the client-side code will be generated for the domain services and the shared code.

To get started using WCF 4.5 RIA Services in Silverlight 5, follow these simple steps:

1. Open **Visual Studio 2013 IDE**.
2. Click on **File** and then **New Project**.

3. Select **Silverlight** from the templates displayed, and save it with a **Name:**, as shown in the following screenshot:

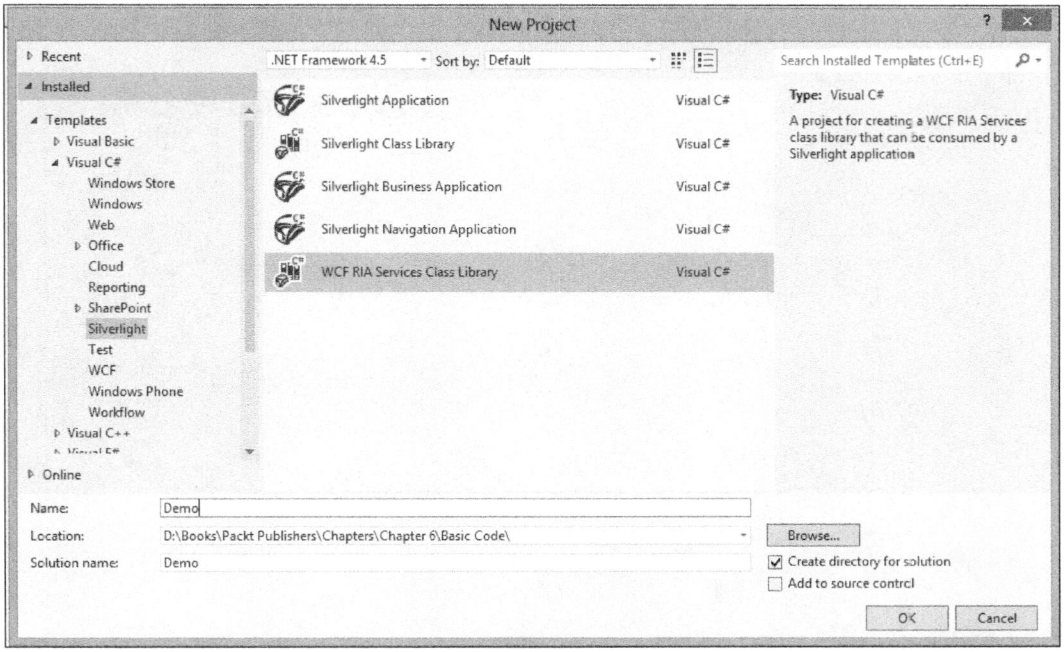

4. Next, delete the `Class1.cs` files in the server and client projects in the **Solution Explorer** window.
5. After you delete the `Class1.cs` file in both the **Server** and **Client** projects, the **Solution Explorer** window would look like this:

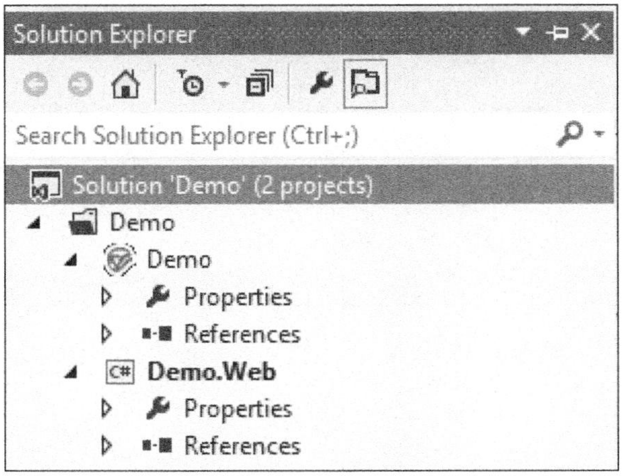

6. Next, right-click on **References** in the **Demo.Web** project, and select **Manage NuGet Packages...** from the menu that is displayed, as shown in the following screenshot:

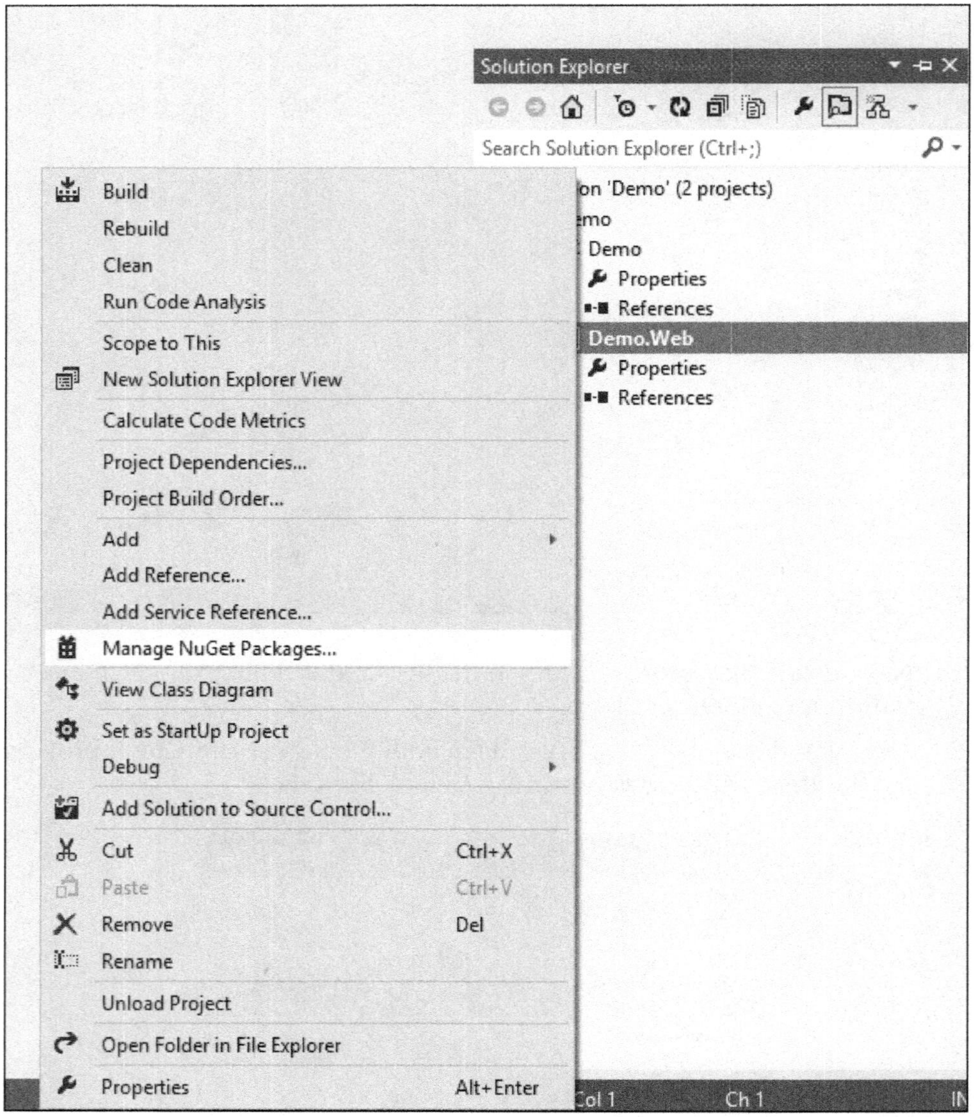

7. From the list of packages **Online** | **All**, you can see **EntityFramework** listed on the next page. Click on **Install**, as shown in the following screenshot:

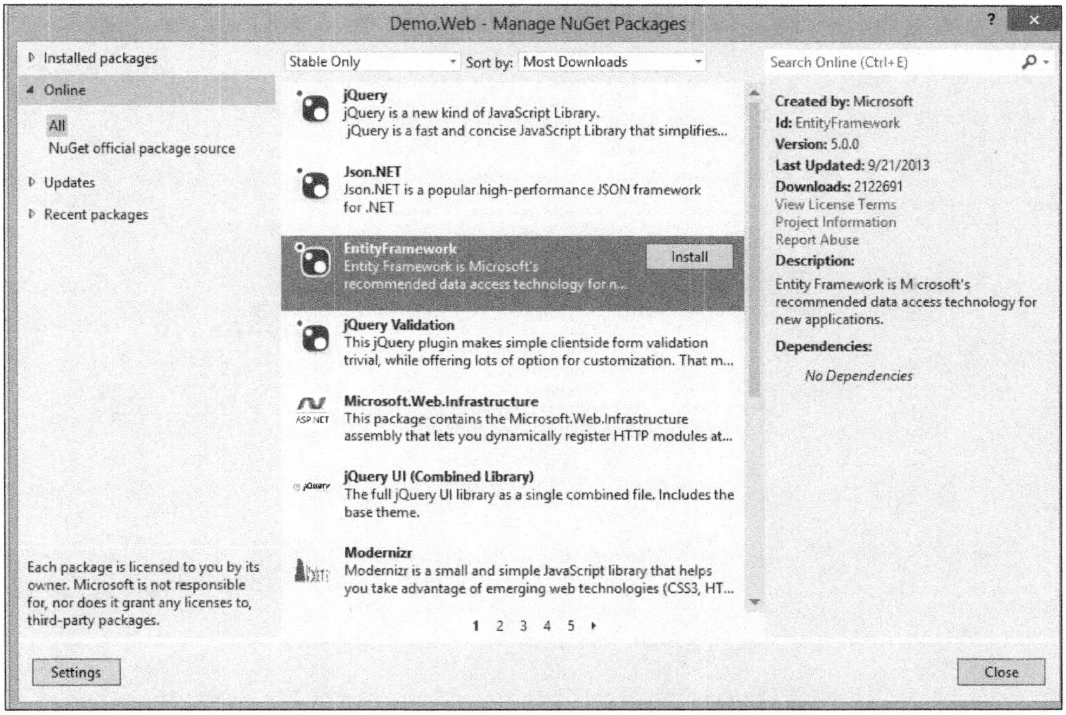

Once you click on **Install**, the installation of Entity Framework will start.

> Note that you can install Entity Framework also by executing commands in the Package Manager Console. You can learn more details about the version of Entity Framework from the NuGet web site: `http://www.nuget.org/packages/entityframework`.

After Entity Framework has been successfully installed, you can see the green tick symbol as shown in the following screenshot:

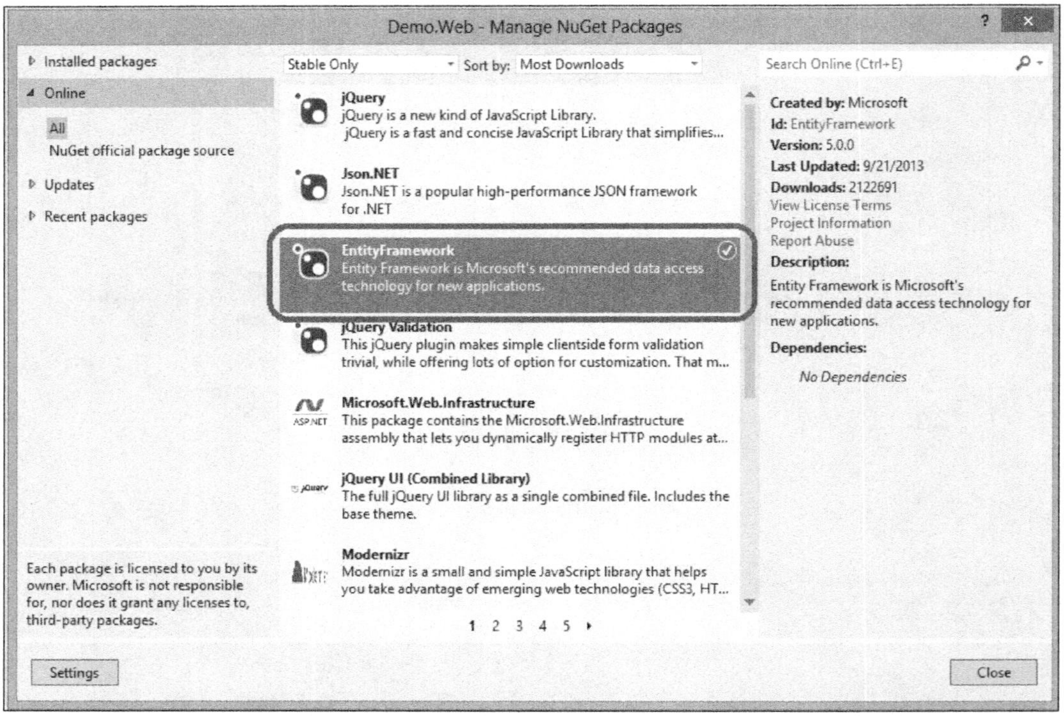

8. Next, create a solution folder named `Models`, and a new entity data model using the `AdventureWorks` database.

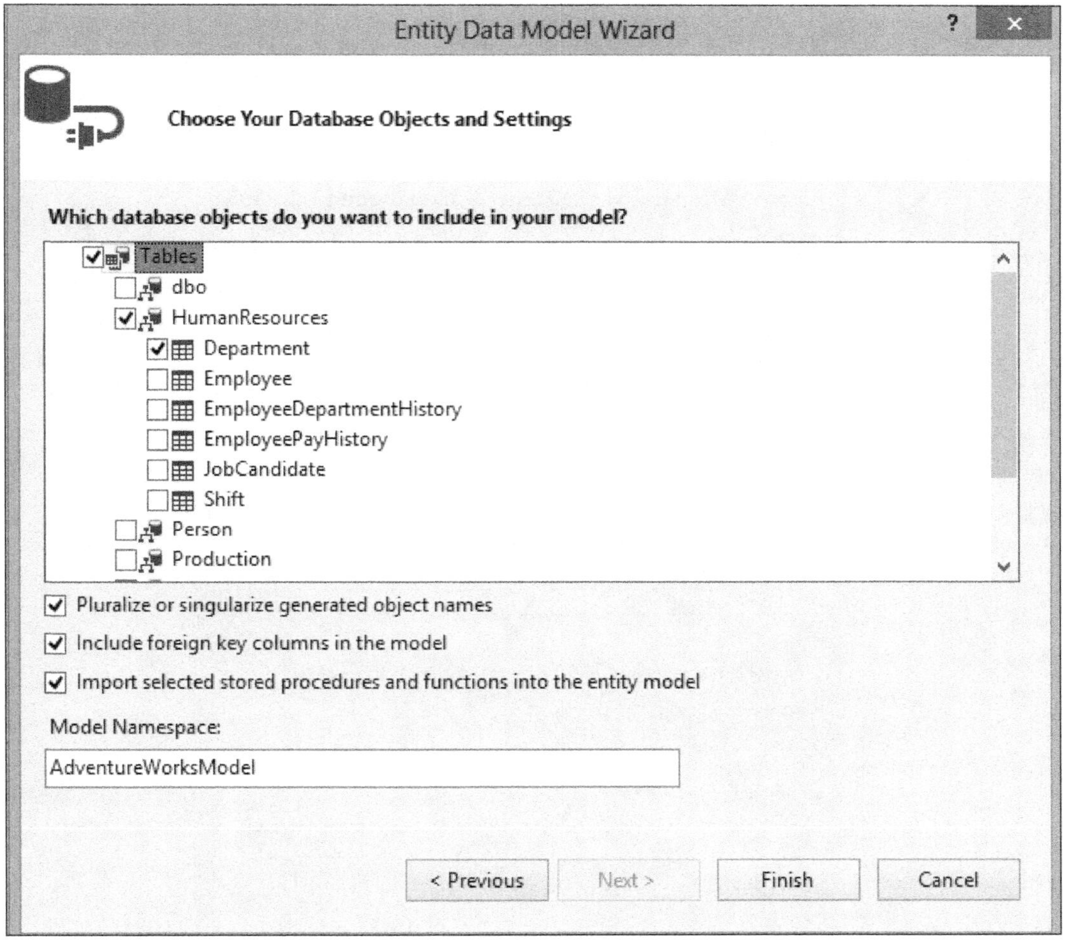

9. Next, create two folders in your web project, one named `App-Code` and the other named `Services`.
10. Now, create a `DomainService` class. To do this, navigate to **Add | New Item** on the `Services` solution folder, and select **Web** from the list of the installed templates. Then select **Domain Service Class**. Name this class `DepartmentDomainService.cs` and, click on **Add**.

If you would like to leverage the Entity Framework entity data model with WCF 4.5 RIA Services, you should convert it to "ObjectContext" based model, otherwise you wouldn't see the entities listed when you are creating the domain service. You would observe a message that states: **Some Entity Framework context classes may have been excluded**.

To overcome this, open your entity data model in the designer mode, and change the **Code Generation Strategy** from **None** to **Default**. Next, delete the two `.tt` files that are adjacent to the model, and then rebuild the project.

11. The next step is to add a domain service class. Refer to the following screenshot:

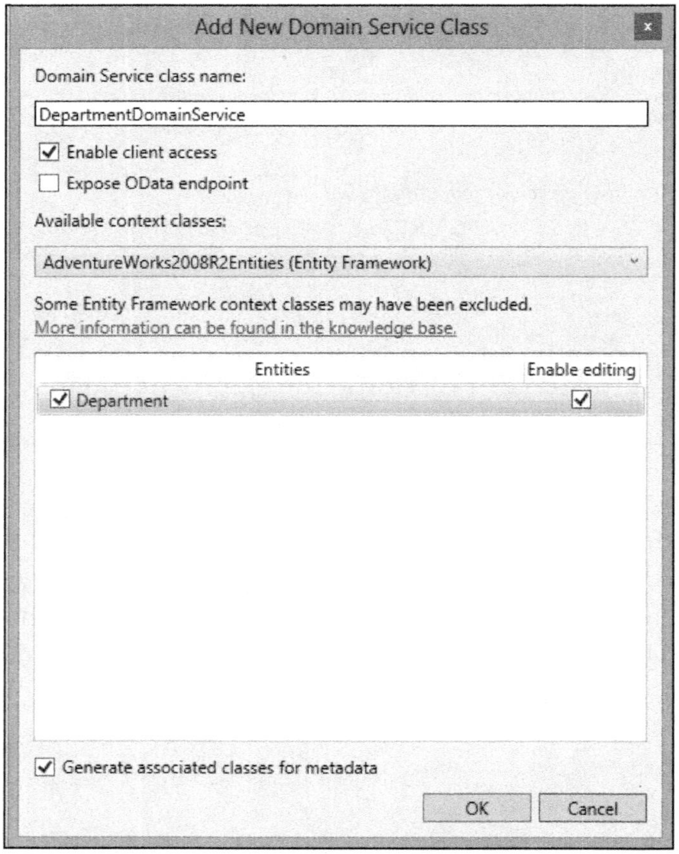

12. When you click on **OK**, the domain service class for the **Department** entity will be created automatically by the framework.

> It should be noted that if you add a class library project to a Silverlight business application project, you are constrained from adding an authentication service to the server project. The reason of this is that the user object in the Silverlight business application template cannot be accessed from the class library project.

It should be noted that Silverlight is incapable of sharing assemblies with the server side. To bridge this gap .NET RIA Services are used. If .NET RIA Services are used, classes that are almost a replica of the domain classes are code generated on the client side. This ensures that you can move objects back and forth between the server side and the client side. The following diagram illustrates how the **RIA Link** is established between a **Silverlight Application** and a **Web Application**, when you use **WCF RIA Services** and consume them using Silverlight:

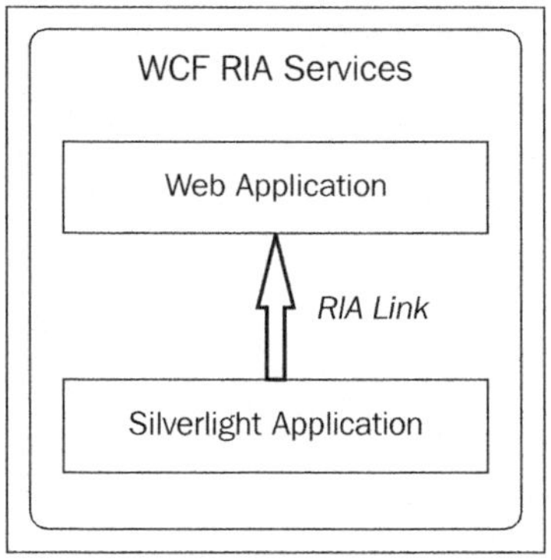

Now let's take a look at the `Domain Service` class that was automatically generated. Here's how the `DepartmentDomainService` class will look like:

```
namespace Demo.Web.Services
{
    using System.Data;
    using System.Linq;
    using System.ServiceModel.DomainServices.EntityFramework;
    using System.ServiceModel.DomainServices.Hosting;
    using Demo.Web.Models;

    [EnableClientAccess()]
    public class DepartmentDomainService :
    LinqToEntitiesDomainService<AdventureWorks2008R2Entities>
    {
        public IQueryable<Department> GetDepartments()
        {
```

```
            return this.ObjectContext.Departments;
        }

        public void InsertDepartment(Department department)
        {
            if ((department.EntityState != EntityState.Detached))
            {
                this.ObjectContext.ObjectStateManager.
                ChangeObjectState(department, EntityState.Added);
            }
            else
            {
                this.ObjectContext.Departments.
                AddObject(department);
            }
        }

        public void UpdateDepartment(Department currentDepartment)
        {
            this.ObjectContext.Departments.AttachAsModified
            (currentDepartment, this.ChangeSet.GetOriginal
            (currentDepartment));
        }

        public void DeleteDepartment(Department department)
        {
            if ((department.EntityState != EntityState.Detached))
            {
                this.ObjectContext.ObjectStateManager.
                ChangeObjectState(department,
                EntityState.Deleted);
            }
            else
            {
                this.ObjectContext.Departments.Attach(department);
                this.ObjectContext.Departments.
                DeleteObject(department);
            }
        }
    }
}
```

Refer to the preceding code snippet. When building LOB applications, common features are create, update, read, and delete operations on the data. The `EnableClientAccessAttribute` attribute in the `System.Web.Ria` namespace enables the client-side code to be generated at the compile time.

You can now specify the necessary configuration to consume the data exposed by this WCF 4.5 RIA Service.

Now, let's quickly create a domain service class based on `SecurityDB` we created earlier in this book.

Follow these steps:

1. Create a new project named `DomainServices`.
2. Create an entity data model based on the **Control** and **ControlType** tables of `SecurityDB` as shown in the following screenshot:

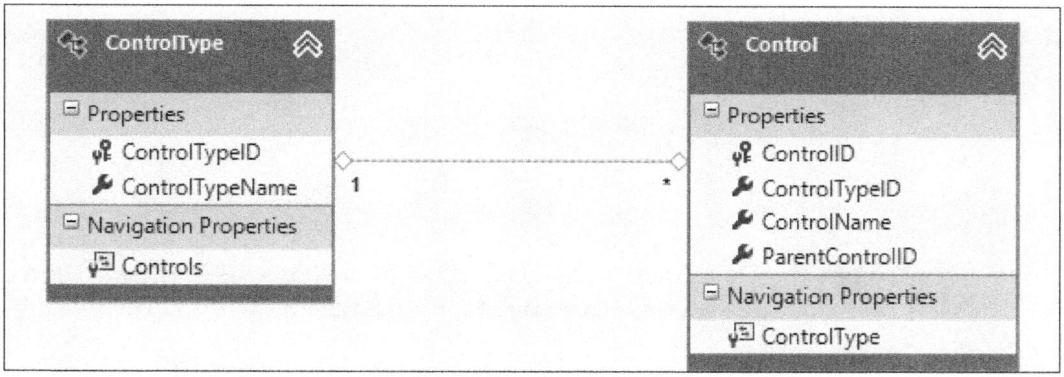

3. Select the newly created project, then right-click and navigate to **Add** | **New Item**.

4. Select **Domain Service Class** from the templates displayed as shown in the following screenshot:

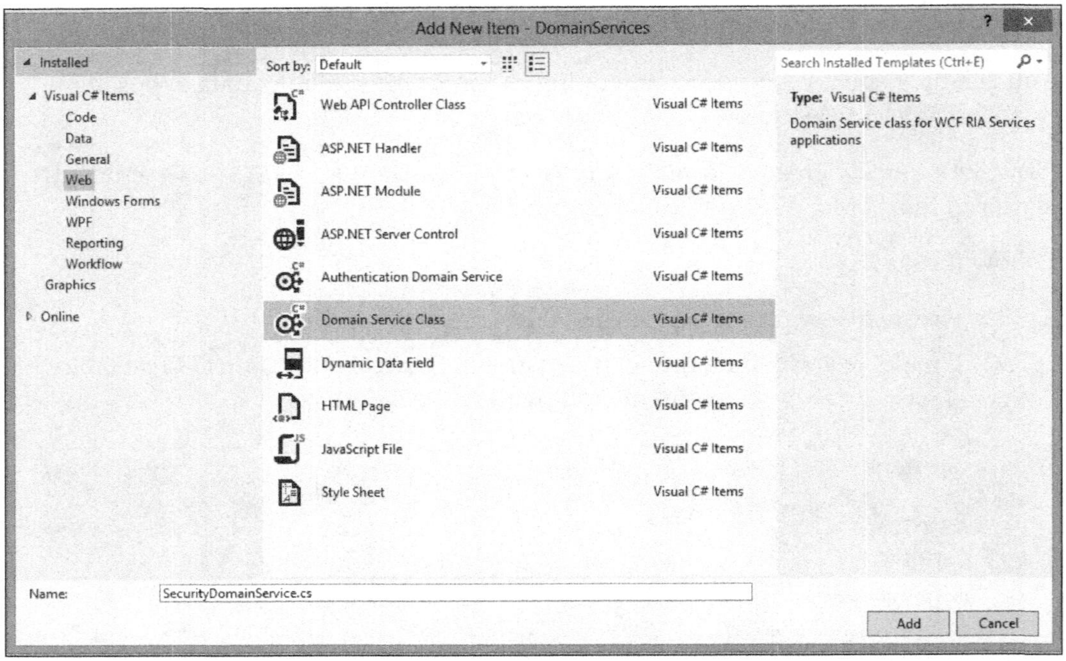

5. Now, name the **Domain Service Class** as `SecurityDomainService.cs` and click on **Add**. You will see a page that looks like the following screenshot:

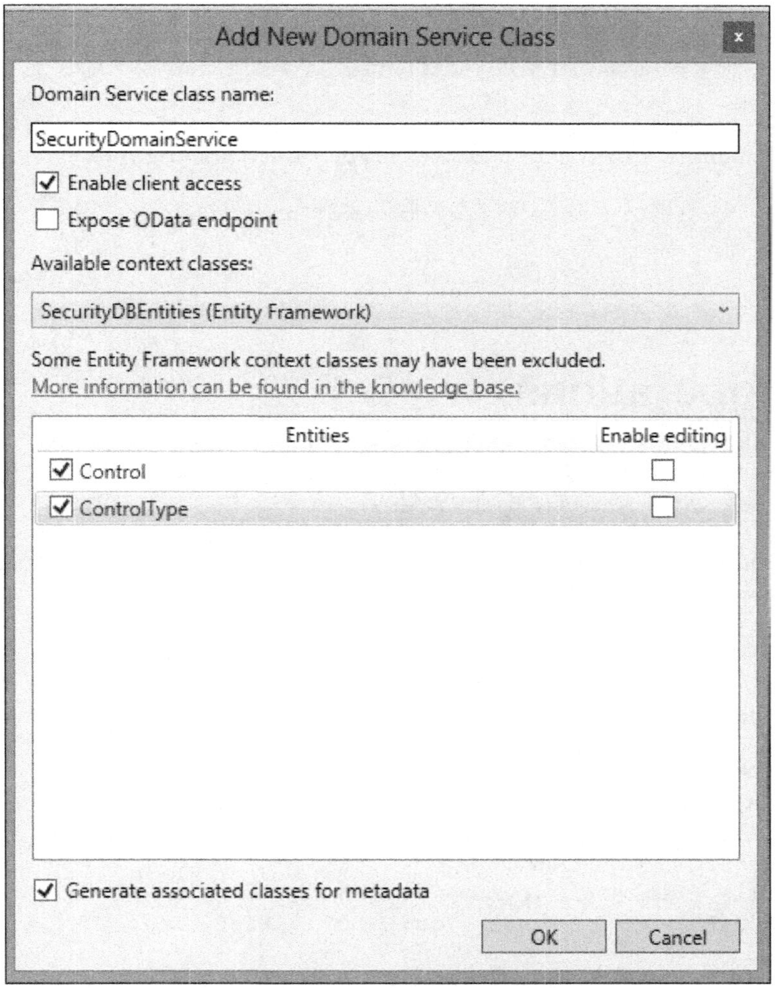

As you can see, two entities **Control** and **ControlType** are listed. Select both of them and click on **OK**. The Domain service Class will now be generated. At first glance, the `SecurityDomainService` class looks like this:

```
namespace DomainServices
{
    using System.Linq;
    using System.ServiceModel.DomainServices.EntityFramework;
    using System.ServiceModel.DomainServices.Hosting;
    [EnableClientAccess()]
    public class SecurityDomainService :
    LinqToEntitiesDomainService<SecurityDBEntities>
    {
```

```
        public IQueryable<Control> GetControls()
        {
            return this.ObjectContext.Controls;
        }

        public IQueryable<ControlType> GetControlTypes()
        {
            return this.ObjectContext.ControlTypes;
        }
    }
}
```

CRUD operations

The next step is to add the necessary CRUD methods to Domain Service for creating a new record, updating an existing record, deleting an existing record, and retrieving one or more records belonging to the `Control` or `ControlType` tables.

Here's the complete code of the `SecurityDomainService` class after the necessary CRUD methods have been added:

```
namespace DomainServices
{
    using System.Data;
    using System.Linq;
    using System.ServiceModel.DomainServices.EntityFramework;
    using System.ServiceModel.DomainServices.Hosting;

    [EnableClientAccess()]
    public class SecurityDomainService :
    LinqToEntitiesDomainService<SecurityDBEntities>
    {
        public IQueryable<Control> GetControls()
        {
            return this.ObjectContext.Controls;
        }

        public IQueryable<ControlType> GetControlTypes()
        {
            return this.ObjectContext.ControlTypes;
        }

        public IQueryable<Control> GetControls()
        {
            return this.ObjectContext.Controls;
        }
```

```
public IQueryable<ControlType> GetControlTypes()
{
    return this.ObjectContext.ControlTypes;
}

public void InsertControl(Control control)
{
    if ((control.EntityState != EntityState.Detached))
    {
        this.ObjectContext.ObjectStateManager.
        ChangeObjectState(control, EntityState.Added);
    }
    else
    {
        this.ObjectContext.Controls.AddObject(control);
    }
}

public void InsertControlType(ControlType controlType)
{
    if ((controlType.EntityState != EntityState.Detached))
    {
        this.ObjectContext.ObjectStateManager.
        ChangeObjectState(controlType, EntityState.Added);
    }
    else
    {
        this.ObjectContext.ControlTypes.
        AddObject(controlType);
    }
}

public void UpdateControls(Control controlObj)
{
    this.ObjectContext.Controls.
    AttachAsModified(controlObj,
    this.ChangeSet.GetOriginal(controlObj));
}

public void UpdateControlTypes(ControlType controlTypeObj)
{
    this.ObjectContext.ControlTypes.
    AttachAsModified(controlTypeObj,
    this.ChangeSet.GetOriginal(controlTypeObj));
}
```

```
        public void DeleteControls(Control controlObj)
        {
            if ((controlObj.EntityState != EntityState.Detached))
            {
                this.ObjectContext.ObjectStateManager.
                ChangeObjectState(controlObj,
                EntityState.Deleted);
            }
            else
            {
                this.ObjectContext.Controls.Attach(controlObj);
                this.ObjectContext.Controls.
                DeleteObject(controlObj);
            }
        }

        public void DeleteControlTypes(ControlType controlTypeObj)
        {
            if ((controlTypeObj.EntityState !=
            EntityState.Detached))
            {
                this.ObjectContext.ObjectStateManager.
                ChangeObjectState(controlTypeObj,
                EntityState.Deleted);
            }
            else
            {
                this.ObjectContext.ControlTypes.
                Attach(controlTypeObj);
                this.ObjectContext.ControlTypes.
                DeleteObject(controlTypeObj);
            }
        }
    }
}
```

To consume the Domain Service from Silverlight 5, you need to follow the same steps as discussed earlier in this chapter.

> Here are a few links for further reference on this topic:
>
> - http://msdn.microsoft.com/en-us/library/gg986857%28v=vs.95%29.aspx
> - http://www.silverlightshow.net/items/WCF-RIA-Services-Part-1-Getting-Started.aspx
> - http://www.johnpapa.net/silverlight5features/
> - http://msdn.microsoft.com/en-us/library/ee707336%28v=vs.91%29.aspx
> - http://code.msdn.microsoft.com/silverlight/Getting-Started-WCF-RIA-1469cbe2
> - http://mtaulty.com/CommunityServer/blogs/mike_taultys_blog/archive/2010/05/04/silverlight-and-wcf-ria-services-1-overview.aspx

Summary

You can use WCF 4.5 RIA Services to write applications that range from small business applications to significantly complex applications. In this chapter, we have discussed WCF 4.5 RIA Services and how they can be consumed from Silverlight 5 applications. In the next chapter, we will discuss some of the advanced features that include the best practices in using WCF Services and ASP.NET Web API.

7
Advanced Features

This is the last chapter of this book, where we will explore some advanced concepts in WCF and Web API.

In this chapter, we will cover the following points:

- Best practices in using WCF services
- Best practices in using ASP.NET Web API

Best practices in using WCF

Windows Communication Foundation (**WCF**) is a unified programming model for building service-oriented applications. WCF provides a powerful framework to design, build, configure, and deploy **SOA** based applications, where SOA stands for **Service Oriented Architecture**.

Microsoft released WCF, initially codenamed *Indigo*, in 2006 as part of .NET Framework 3.0.

WCF enables developers to build secure, reliable, and transacted solutions that integrate across different platforms and provides a high degree of interoperability with existing investments.

The core philosophy of WCF can be boiled down to the following three key concepts commonly known as ABC:

- Address
- Binding
- Contract

In this section, we will explore the best practices to consider when creating applications using WCF.

WCF security issues

In this section, we will explore how we can implement a robust security for our WCF services. We will start our discussion with a brief introduction to WCF bindings.

Bindings

A binding is used to specify the transport channel (HTTP, TCP, pipes, and Message Queuing) and the protocols (Security, Reliability, and Transaction flows). A binding comprises of binding elements, and also includes message encoding elements (text/XML, MTOM, and binary). These binding elements denote how an endpoint communicates with service consumers. WCF provides support for nine built-in bindings. A binding must include at least one transport binding element, one encoding binding element, and one or more other transport protocol bindings, such as security and reliability. Note that the binding information that needs to be specified in the server and the client is different; that is, you have to specify the binding information in the configuration file of your WCF service and also in the configuration file in the WCF service client.

In WCF, the three major sections in WCF configuration scheme are ServiceModel, bindings, and services.

In essence, binding is an attribute of an endpoint, and you can use it to configure the transport protocol, encoding, and security specifications of a service. Now, which is the binding I should use and when? Here's the rule of thumb:

- `WsHttpBinding`: You can use this type of binding if you need to expose your service over the Internet.
- `basicHttpBinding`: You should select this type of binding if you need to expose your WCF service to legacy clients, such as an ASMX web service. One of the major differences between `WsHttpBinding` and `basicHttpBinding` is in message security.
- `WsFederationHttpBinding`: This is a special type of of WS binding that offers support for federated security.
- `NetTcpBinding`: You can use this type of binding if you need to support WCF clients within an intranet. This is the most optimized and fastest binding available, and supports reliability, transactions, and security. `NetTcpBinding` provides support for TCP protocol and both the binary as well as encoding methods.

- `NetPeerTcpBinding`: This binding provides support for the features of `netTcpBinding`, and is much more secure for a peer-to-peer environment that uses WCF services.
- `netNamedPipeBinding`: This type of binding is a good choice if you need to support WCF clients on the same machine.
- `netMsmqBinding`: You can select this type of binding if you need to support disconnected queued calls.
- `wsDualHttpBinding`: You can select this type of binding if you would like to provide support for bidirectional communication between the service and the client. This type of binding has all the features of `WsHttpBinding`; in addition, it provides support for the Duplex **Message Exchange Pattern** (**MEP**).

The following table provides a comparison of the bindings in WCF:

Binding	**Configuration**	**Protocol/ Transport**	**Security**	**Transaction**	**Duplex**
BasicHttpBinding	Basic Profile 1.1	HTTP/HTTPS	None	...	...
WSHttpBinding	WS	HTTP, HTTPS, TCP	Message	Yes	...
WSDualHttp Binding	WS	HTTP, HTTPS	Message	Yes	Yes
NetTcpBinding	.NET	Named pipe	Transport	Yes	Yes
NetNamedPipe Binding	.NET	Named pipe	Transport	Yes	Yes
NetMsmqBinding	.NET	MSMQ	Transport	Yes	No
WSFederationHttp Binding	WS-federation	HTTP, HTTPS	Message	Yes	No
NetPeerTcpBinding	Peer	TCP	Transport	...	Yes
MsmqIntegration Binding	MSMQ	MSMQ	Transport	Yes	...

> You can also have `Custom` binding that allows creating a custom binding using a combination of different binding elements.

WCF security

Confidentiality and integrity of data and information is of utmost importance when you are using WCF services. You create service operations and then expose them to the outer world. There are various ways in which you can secure your WCF services, which are as follows:

- Using authentication
- Using authorization
- Using certificates
- Using transport level security
- Using message level security
- Using token-based security

Additionally, you can provide security in WCF at two levels. You can either provide the security at the transport level or at the message level. Now, there are pros and cons of both these levels.

Transport security is transport dependent. It provides interoperability and improved performance, and should be used when the message that you send is routed through intermediate systems, and both the service and the client are located in an intranet network. However, transport security provides minimum support for credentials when compared to message security.

Message-level security

In message-level security, the credentials of the user are encapsulated with the message that is passed between the server and the client. Message security is suitable when the message needs to be forwarded to other WCF services or routed through intermediate systems. However, message security is slow in comparison to transport security, because of the overhead needed to encrypt and sign every message. Also, message security doesn't support interoperability with older ASMX clients. The credential types that message security supports are Windows, None, Certificate, User Name, and Token.

The following code snippet illustrates how you can implement message-level security by securing a message using the `wsHttpBinding` binding:

```
<wsHttpBinding>
  <binding name = "wsHttp">
    <security mode = "Message">
      <message clientCredentialType = "UserToken"/>
    </security>
  </binding>
</wsHttpBinding>
```

If you are using certificate security in the message security mode, here's how you can secure your WCF services:

```
<bindings>
  <wsHttpBinding>
    <binding name="wsHttpEndpointBinding">
      <security>
        <message clientCredentialType="Certificate" />
      </security>
    </binding>
  </wsHttpBinding>
</bindings>
```

> To specify message security protection levels on the interface or operation level, you have to make use of the `[ServiceContract(ProtectionLevel)]` attribute and set the protection level. You can choose from any of the supported protection levels, that is, `None`, `Sign`, and `EncryptAndSign`.

Implement message-level security in WCF 4.5 with the following steps:

1. Create certificates for both the server and the client (service provider and service consumer) using the `makecert.exe` tool.
2. Using Visual Studio 2013 IDE, create a WCF application.
3. Specify the necessary binding behavior in the configuration file for the server, as shown in the following code:

```
<bindings>
  <wsHttpBinding>
    <binding name="wsHttpEndpointBinding">
      <security>
        <message clientCredentialType="Certificate" />
      </security>
    </binding>
  </wsHttpBinding>
</bindings>

<serviceCredentials>
  <clientCertificate>
    <authentication certificateValidationMode="PeerTrust"/>
  </clientCertificate>
  <serviceCertificate findValue="DemoWCFServer"
    storeLocation="CurrentUser"
    storeName="My"
    x509FindType="FindBySubjectName" />
</serviceCredentials>
```

4. Create the WCF client application, and configure the client certificate credentials, as shown in the following code:

```
<behaviors>
  <endpointBehaviors>
    <behavior name="CustomBehavior">
      <clientCredentials>
        <clientCertificate findValue="DemoWCFClient"
          x509FindType="FindBySubjectName"
          storeLocation="CurrentUser" storeName="My" />
        <serviceCertificate>
          <authentication
            certificateValidationMode="PeerTrust"/>
        </serviceCertificate>
      </clientCredentials>
    </behavior>
  </endpointBehaviors>
</behaviors>
<client>
  <endpoint address="http://localhost:1234/
    DemoService.svc" binding="wsHttpBinding"
    bindingConfiguration="WSEndpoint"
      contract="Packt.Services.IDemoService"
    name="WSEndpoint"
      behaviorConfiguration="CustomBehavior">
    <identity>
      <dns value="DemoWCFServer"/>
    </identity>
  </endpoint>
</client>
```

And you are done!

Using the FaultContract attribute

The following code snippet creates an interface with the protection level set to `Sign`:

```
[ServiceContract(ProtectionLevel=ProtectionLevel.Sign]
  public interface ISecurityService
  {
    [OperationContract]
    [FaultContract(typeof(FaultDetails))]
    UserLoginHistory GetUserLoginHistory(Int32 userID);
  }
```

The `FaultContractAttribute` class is used to specify one or more SOAP defaults that are returned when a call to a service method encounters an error at runtime. The following code snippet specifies an operation with the protection level set to `Sign`:

```
[OperationContract(ProtectionLevel=ProtectionLevel.Sign]
```

The `GetUserLoginInformation` service method returns the login history details of the user, whose user ID is passed as a parameter.

The `SecurityService` class implements the `ISecurityService` interface (the service contract) and defines the `getUserLoginInformation` method (the operation contract). The following code snippet shows how the `SecurityService` class looks:

```
public class SecurityService : ISecurityService
  {
    public UserLoginHistory GetUserLoginHistory(Int32 userID)
    {
      try
      {
        return new UserLoginHistory { UserID = userID };
      }
      catch
      {
        FaultDetails faultObject = new FaultDetails();
        faultObject.FaultID = 1;
        faultObject.FaultMessage = "The User ID you
          entered is invalid...";

        throw new FaultException<FaultDetails> (faultObject,
          new FaultReason(faultObject.FaultMessage));
      }
    }
  }
```

As you can see in the previous code snippet, the `GetUserLoginHistory` operation contract returns an instance of `UserLoginHistory`. I've skipped the code to retrieve the user login history for the user ID passed as a parameter.

We would need two message contracts, one for storing the user's login history, and the other for the fault details when a fault exception occurs. The `MessageBodyMemberAttribute` class belongs to .NET Framework 4.5, and is used to specify that a member is serialized as an element inside the SOAP body.

The following code snippet is the code for the two message contracts that we would need to use:

```
[MessageContract]
public class UserLoginHistory
{
  [MessageBodyMemberAttribute(Order = 1, ProtectionLevel =
    ProtectionLevel.None)]
  public Int32 UserID { get; set; }

  [MessageBodyMemberAttribute(Order = 2, ProtectionLevel =
    ProtectionLevel.Sign)]
  public DateTime LoginTime { get; set; }

  [MessageBodyMemberAttribute(Order = 2, ProtectionLevel =
    ProtectionLevel.EncryptAndSign)]
  public DateTime Password { get; set; }
}

[MessageContract]
public class FaultDetails
{
  [MessageBodyMemberAttribute(Order = 1, ProtectionLevel =
    ProtectionLevel.None)]
  public Int32 FaultID
  {
    get;
    set;
  }

  [MessageBodyMemberAttribute(Order = 2, ProtectionLevel =
    ProtectionLevel.None)]
  public string FaultMessage
  {
    get;
    set;
  }
}
```

After the service reference has been added, you can consume the service from the client application using the following code:

```
try
{
  ChannelFactory<ISecurityService> factory =
  new ChannelFactory<
    ISecurityService>("WSHttpBinding_ISecurityService",
  new EndpointAddress("
    http://localhost/Packt/SecurityService.svc"));
```

```
    ISecurityService proxy = factory.CreateChannel();
    UserLoginHistory userLoginHistoryObj =
      proxy.GetUserLoginHistory(3);
  }
  catch (FaultException<FaultDetails> faultExceptionInstance)
  {
    //Some code
  }
```

> You can turn off security in WCF programmatically. An example of that is as follows:
>
> ```
> bindingObject.Security.Mode = SecurityMode.None;
> ```

Transport-level security

Transport security works much faster in comparison to message security, and the transport-level security is protocol independent.

The available client credential types you can use when you are implementing the `basicHttpBinding` or `WsHttpBinding` binding in the transport security mode include the following:

- **None**: No security; security is turned off
- **Basic**: Basic authentication works only with the HTTP protocol. Here, the client is authenticated against the active directory
- **Digest**: This type of authentication is similar to Basic, but in this option, the credentials are sent as a hash, instead of clear text
- **NTLM**: This also works only with the HTTP protocol, and clients are authenticated using Windows accounts
- **Windows**: In this option, a Windows token is used to authenticate against the active directory
- **Certificate**: In this option, a service is authenticated using the service certificate or an SSL certificate if the protocol in use is HTTP

Implementing transport-level security

The following code snippet illustrates how you can implement transport security using the following code:

```
NetTcpBinding netTcpBinding = new
  NetTcpBinding(SecurityMode.TransportWithMessageCredential);
netTcpBinding.Security.Transport.ClientCredentialType =
  TcpClientCredentialType.Windows;
```

```
netTcpBinding.Security.Message.ClientCredentialType =
  MessageCredentialType.Certificate;
Uri adddress = new Uri("net.tcp://Tcp");
ServiceHost serviceHost = new ServiceHost(typeof(
  SecurityService), adddress);
serviceHost.Credentials.ServiceCertificate.SetCertificate(
  StoreLocation.LocalMachine, StoreName.My,
  X509FindType.FindByIssuerName, "Contoso.com");
serviceHost.AddServiceEndpoint(typeof(ISecurityService),
  b, "SecurityService");
serviceHost.Open();
Console.WriteLine("Service Started.........");
Console.ReadOLine();
```

> Note that by default, `netTcpBinding` uses transport security. This implies that you should configure the client credentials to use certificate security.

To implement transport-level security through configuration, you should specify the security mode in the configuration file, as shown in the following code snippet:

```
<bindings>
  <wsHttpBinding>
    <binding name="TransportSecurity">
      <security mode="Transport">
        <transport clientCredentialType="None"/>
      </security>
    </binding>
  </wsHttpBinding>
</bindings>
```

> To use `netTcpBinding` with Windows for transport security, you can use the following code:

```
<bindings>
  <netTcpBinding>
    <binding name="PacktTcpBinding">
      <security mode="TransportWithMessageCredential" >
        <transport clientCredentialType="Windows" />
        <message clientCredentialType="Certificate" />
      </security>
    </binding>
  </netTcpBinding>
</bindings>
```

If you use HTTPS protocol, you should change `httpGetEnabled` to `httpsGetEnabled` on the service behavior, as shown in the following code snippet:

```
<behaviors>
  <serviceBehaviors>
    <behavior name="Packt.SecureService.SecurityServiceBehavior">
      <!-- To avoid disclosing metadata information, set the value
        below to false and remove the metadata endpoint above
        before deployment -->
      <serviceMetadata httpsGetEnabled="true"/>
      <!-- To receive exception details in faults for debugging
        purposes, set the value below to true.  Set to false
        before deployment to avoid disclosing exception
        information -->
      <serviceDebug includeExceptionDetailInFaults="false"/>
    </behavior>
  </serviceBehaviors>
</behaviors>
```

The next step is to specify the end points to support the secure communication. Please refer to the following code:

```
<services>
  <service name="Packt.SecureService.SecurityService"
    behaviorConfiguration="Packt.SecureService.
    SecurityServiceBehavior" >
    <!-- Service Endpoints -->
    <endpoint address="http://localhost/Packt/SecurityService.svc"
      binding="wsHttpBinding" bindingConfiguration="
      TransportSecurity" contract="
      Packt.SecureService.ISecurityService"/>
    <endpoint address="mex" binding="mexHttpsBinding" contract="
      IMetadataExchange"/>
  </service>
</services>
```

Now you should host your service in IIS. To do this, right-click on the service project in the solution explorer window, and in the **Web** tab, select the **Use Local IIS Web Server** radio button shown in the following screenshot:

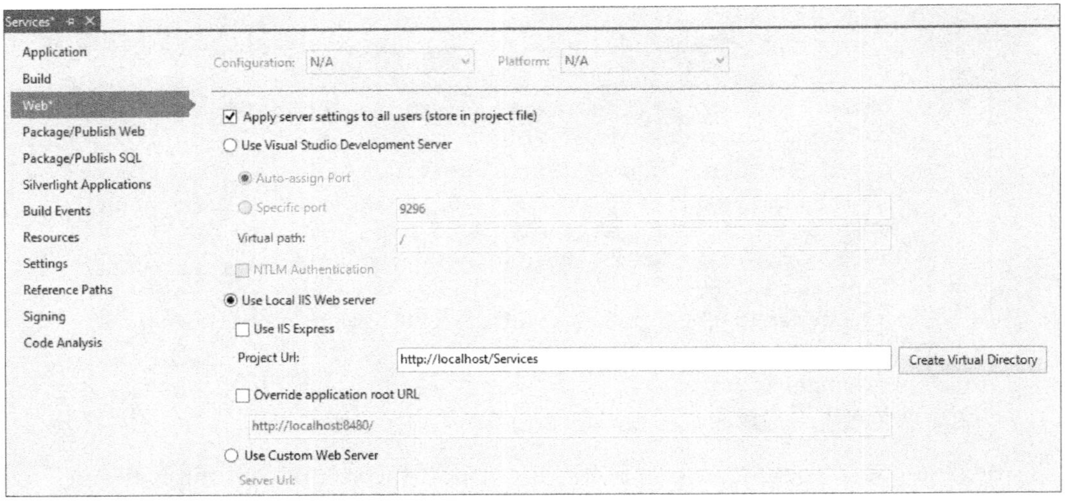

You should also create a virtual directory by clicking on the **Create Virtual Directory** button, as shown in the preceding screenshot. The next screen looks like this:

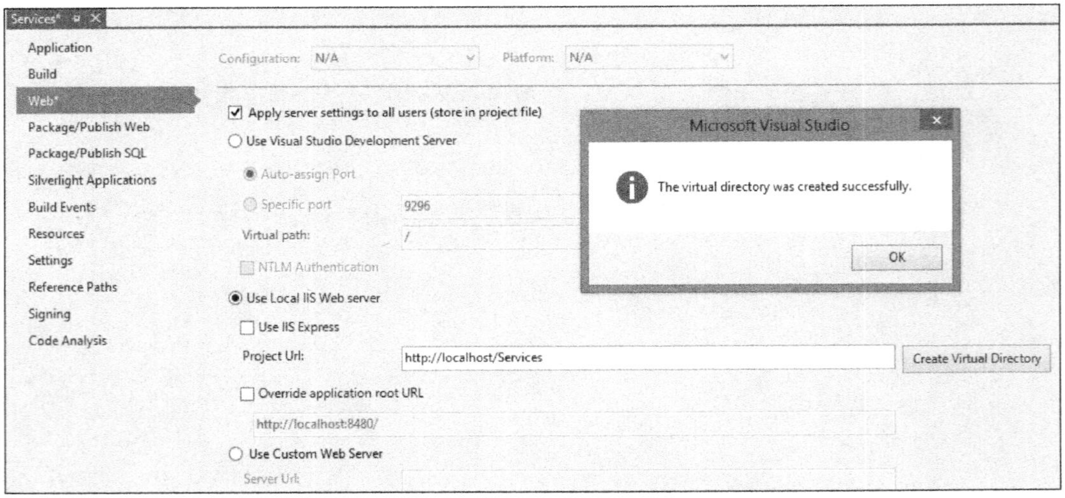

Note that in order to host a service in IIS from Visual Studio IDE, you should open the Visual Studio 2012 IDE in administrator mode.

You can then go to the **Internet Services Manager** window and associate an SSL certificate to the website. You should also turn on SSL bindings for your website.

Best practices in using WCF services

Here are a few points you should keep in mind while using WCF services:

- Don't put proxies in a `using` statement.
- Use the `FaultExceptions` class for handling service exceptions. You should use the `FaultContracts` class to return error information to the service consumers.
- Use message logging to log service operations.
- It is always preferable to use a per call instance model.
- Use WCF tools, such as `SvcUtil.exe`, `SvcConfigEditor.exe`, and `SvcTraceViewer.exe`.
- You should protect logfiles from unauthorized access, and the logfiles should not contain sensitive information.
- Use a proper authentication mechanism to authenticate service consumers.
- Use string passwords, and protect access to the credential store.
- Use IIS to host your service, unless you would like to use a transport protocol that is not supported by IIS.
- Validate input parameters on the server side, and don't rely on client-side validation only.
- Define maintainable services and data contract versioning.
- Define your namespaces clearly to avoid conflict.
- Encrypt configuration sections that contain sensitive data.
- You should manage binding and endpoint information through configuration, and not through code.
- Define services in a class library, and not directly in a host project.
- Include the `FaultContract` attribute in the service contract definition.
- Use static proxy classes instead of the `ChannelFactory` class.
- Use the Cache to store client proxies if you have to call service methods frequently.
- Use X509 certificates instead of NTLM.
- You should publish metadata only after securing the metadata exchange endpoint with transport or message-level security.

- You should favor data contracts over serializable types.
- Use WAS hosting wherever possible and IIS hosting for external HTTP-only services.
- You can use Protocol Buffer WCF services for better performance. You can learn more about Protocol Buffers and how you can use them in WCF services at `http://www.developer.com/net/net/working-with-protobuf-services-in-.net.html`.

Best practices in using the ASP.NET Web API

ASP.NET Web API is an ideal platform for building RESTful applications on the .NET framework. The ASP.NET Web API is a framework that can be used to build `Http` services regardless of `REST` or `RPC`—it is Microsoft's best implementation of RFC. It allows both IIS and self hosting, and is asynchronous. The Web API is flexible and provides support for separation of concerns. It enables you to expose applications, data, and services to the Web directly over the HTTP protocol. The ASP.NET Web API relies on basic protocol and formats, such as HTTP, WebSockets, SSL, JQuery, JSON, and XML. There is no support for higher level protocols, such as Reliable Messaging or Transactions.

Here's a quick glance at the best practices and tips that you can follow when using the Web API:

- You should use a custom base WebApiController where you can abstract the controller features and behavior
- Use a URL helper for filtering all the image URLs
- Always install the **MvcRoutingShim** plugin to avoid subtle and confusing behavior with multiple HTTP modules
- It is advisable to create a separate controller for each resource

The following code is a quick look at the Base API controller for the Web API we created earlier in this book. The `BaseApiController` class extends the `ApiController` class, and implements the `IBaseApiController` interface.

```
public interface IBaseApiController : IDisposable
{
  Int32 ID { get; set; }
}

public class BaseApiController<T> : ApiController where T :
  class, IBaseApiController
```

```
{
  BaseRepository<SecurityEntities> repository = null;
  protected string[] includesArray { get; set; }
  public BaseApiController()
  {
    repository = new BaseRepository<SecurityEntities>("
      SecurityEntities");
  }

  public virtual IEnumerable<T> Get()
  {
    return repository.GetData<T>(includesArray);
  }

  public virtual T Get(Int32 id)
  {
    return repository.SearchData<T>(t => t.ID == id,
      includesArray);
  }

  public virtual Int32 Post([FromBody]T value)
  {
    return repository.EditData<T>(value);
  }

  public virtual Int32 Put([FromBody]T value)
  {
    return repository.CreateData<T>(value);
  }

  public virtual Int32 Delete([FromBody]T value)
  {
    return repository.RemoveData<T>(value);
  }
}
```

References

http://msdn.microsoft.com/en-us/magazine/cc163394.aspx

http://msdn.microsoft.com/en-us/library/ms732362.aspx

http://msdn.microsoft.com/en-us/library/ms733099.aspx

http://msdn.microsoft.com/en-us/magazine/cc163382.aspx

http://msdn.microsoft.com/en-us/library/ff405740.aspx

http://www.codemag.com/article/0611051

http://wcf.codeplex.com/wikipage?title=WCF%20HTTP

Summary

WCF provides a platform for the unification of a number of technologies under one single umbrella. It can be used to design and implement platform-independent, extendable, and scalable services. ASP.NET Web API is a lightweight web-based framework that uses HTTP as the application protocol. In this chapter, we discussed the best practices that can be adopted for WCF services and the Web API for enhanced security, scalability, and performance.

Library References

This appendix is organized into two sections, *Section A* and *Section B*.

In *Section A*, we will explore the following:

- Popular REST-based service frameworks/APIs:
    - Ruby on Rails
    - Restlet
    - Django
    - Flickr
    - Google
    - Yahoo!
- Working with Visual Studio 2013 IDE

In *Section B*, we will discuss the following points:

- HTTP response codes
- The ASP.NET Web API class library

Section A

This is Section A of this appendix. We will start our discussion in this section with the popular REST-based service frameworks.

Popular REST-based service frameworks

Representational state transfer is an architectural paradigm. The key goals of REST include the following:

- Scalability
- Compatibility with other technology and platforms
- Generality of interfaces
- Discoverability; that is, interconnectivity between resources
- Components can be deployed independent of one another
- Reduced latency
- Better security
- Extensibility

A RESTful Web API is a web API that conforms to the REST principles. The main principles of REST include:

- Identification of resources
- Stateless communication
- Manipulation of resources through representations
- Self-descriptive messages

The following sections will explain the popular REST-based service frameworks or APIs.

Ruby on Rails

Ruby on Rails is an optimized open source web application framework that runs on top of the Ruby programming language. Ruby on Rails follows the basic software engineering patterns and principles. The Rails Web API is a framework that facilitates the creation of web applications based on the **Model-View-Controller** (**MVC**) framework. The View layer is composed of templates and most of these templates are HTML-based with embedded Ruby code. The Model layer represents the domain model, the business logic classes, and the data access classes. The Controller layer handles incoming HTTP requests. Note that the Rails controller can generate XML, JSON, PDFs, and also mobile-specific views. You can get more information on this framework from `http://api.rubyonrails.org/`.

Restlet

Restlet provides support for an extensive list of extensions that include the following:

- Spring
- WADL
- XML
- JSON
- JAX-RS API

The benefits of Restlet include the following:

- Support for a fully symmetric client/server API
- Support for connector protocols other than HTTP
- Support for complete URI routing control through the Restlet API
- It is fast and scalable
- Powerful filtering support
- Support for a consistent client/server API

You can explore more on this API from `http://restlet.org/discover/features`.

Django REST

The Django REST Framework provides a powerful and flexible API using which you can build Web APIs seamlessly. This API provides an extensive documentation and an excellent community support. You can know more on this framework from this link: `http://django-rest-framework.org/`.

The Flickr REST API

The Flickr REST API is simple and easy to use. Flickr also has some JSON APIs that you might make use of for invoking the API through JavaScript. You can get more information in this regard from `http://www.flickr.com/services/api/request.rest.html`.

The Google API

The Custom Search JSON/Atom API from Google enables developers to write applications that can leverage this API and retrieve and display custom search in the applications. This API allows you to use RESTful calls for web search and get the results in the JSON or Atom format. You can know more on this API from this `https://developers.google.com/custom-search/json-api/v1/overview`.

Yahoo! Social REST APIs

The Yahoo! REST APIs provide a collection of URI resources that can provide access to the following:

- Users' profiles
- Status messages
- Status updates

These URIs are actually grouped into APIs depending on the information they return. For more information, you can refer to the following site: `http://developer.yahoo.com/social/rest_api_guide/web-services-intro.html`.

Section B

In *Section B*, we will explore about working with Visual Studio 2013 IDE.

Working with the Visual Studio 2013 IDE

In this section we will explore how we can work with Visual Studio 2013 IDE. We will first start this section with a discussion on how we can install and set up Visual Studio 2013 IDE in our system.

Installing Visual Studio 2013

In this section we will learn about installing Visual Studio 2013. Visual Studio 2013 RC is now available for download. Here's the link: `http://www.microsoft.com/visualstudio/eng/2013-downloads`.

After you download the setup file, double-click the file to start the installation.

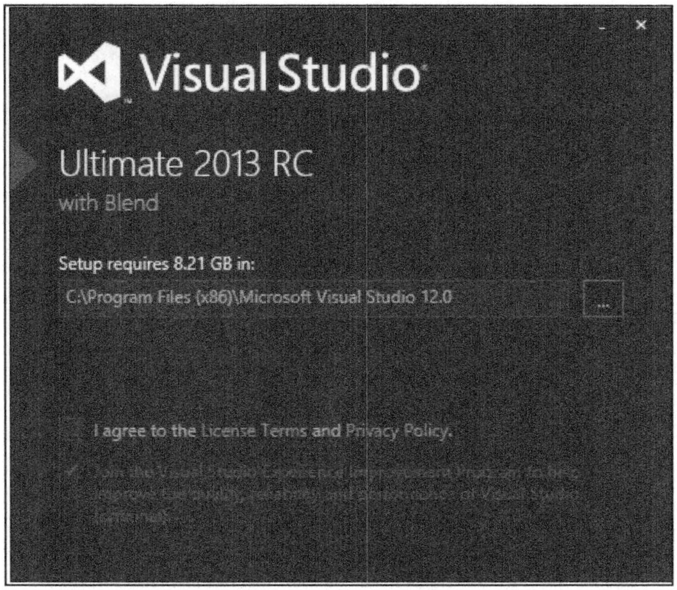

Next, agree to the license terms and privacy policy to move ahead with the installation, as shown in the following screenshot:

When the installation starts, here's what the screen will look like:

After the installation is complete, here is what the screen will look like:

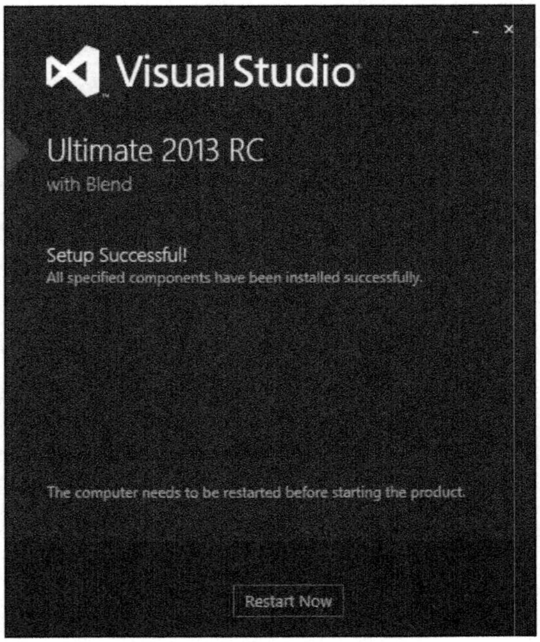

Click on the **Restart Now** button to restart your system and complete the installation of Visual Studio 2013.

Here is what the opening screen of Visual Studio 2013 looks like:

Once you invoke Visual Studio 2013, you will observe that it asks for whether you would like to sign in, as shown in the following screenshot. I selected the option **Not now, maybe later**.

Next, select your **Development Settings:**, as shown in the following screenshot. I selected the **General** option in my system.

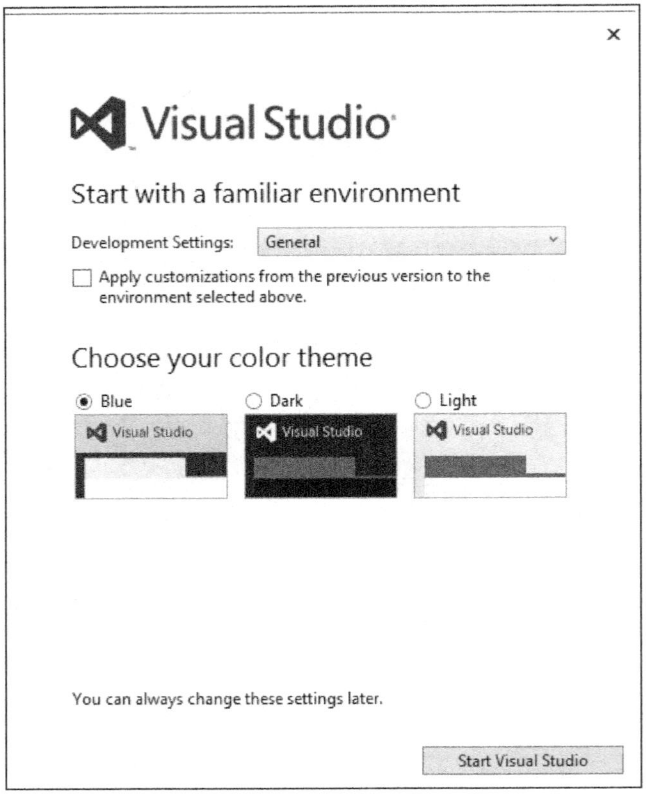

Then, click on the **Start Visual Studio** button. Visual Studio 2013 will now start the necessary preparations/configuration checks for first time usage in your system, as shown in the following screenshot:

Once this process is complete, here is what your Visual Studio 2013 IDE would look like at the first glance:

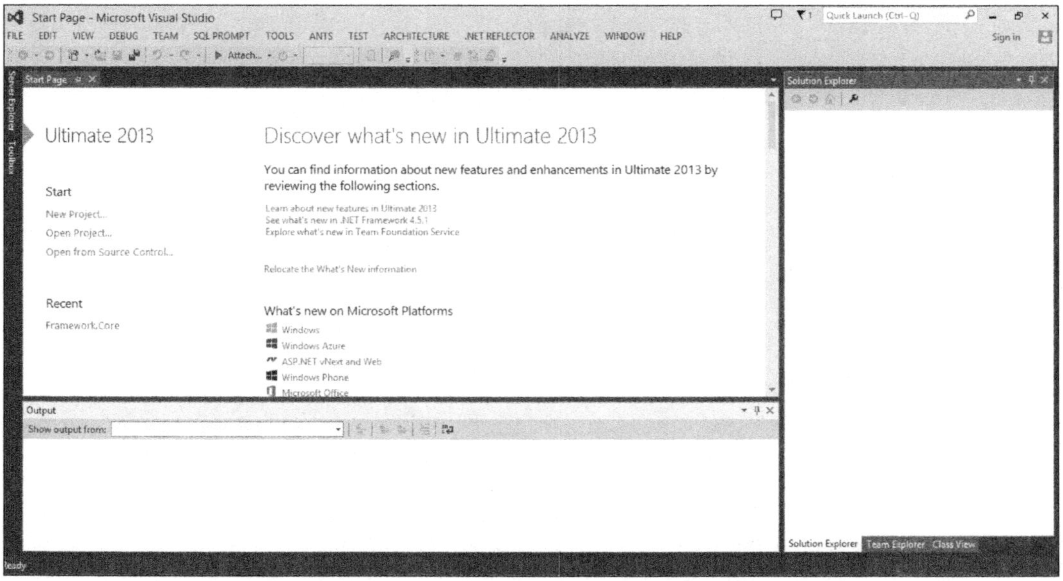

New features in the Visual Studio 2013 IDE

The new features in Visual Studio 2013 IDE include:

- Support for asynchronous debugging
- Support for graphics diagnostics
- Enhanced code editor features
- Support for creating code maps from the code window
- Support for mapping call stack within the debugging mode
- Expanded ALM capabilities
- New IDE features for JavaScript
- Support for creating modern business apps for Office 365
- Support for Windows 8.1 app development
- Enhanced Windows Azure support including Windows Azure Mobile Services

HTTP requests and response code

The following table lists the standard HTTP status codes and their uses. To get the complete information, please refer to the following link:

`http://www.w3.org/Protocols/rfc2616/rfc2616-sec10.html`

Status Code	Description
100	Informational
200	Successful
201	Created
202	Accepted
204	No content
300	Redirection
304	Not modified
400	Client error
401	Unauthorized
402	Payment required
403	Forbidden
404	Not found
405	Method not allowed

Status Code	Description
409	Conflict
500	Server error
501	Not implemented

Abbreviations

- **HTTP**: Hypertext Transfer Protocol
- **ROA**: Resource-Oriented Architectures
- **SOA**: Service-Oriented Architectures
- **SOAP**: Simple Object Access Protocol
- **REST**: Representational State Transfer
- **RPC**: Remote Procedure Call
- **URL**: Uniform Resource Locator
- **W3C**: World Wide Web Consortium
- **WSDL**: Web Service Description Language
- **XML-RPC**: XML Remote Procedure Call

The ASP.NET Web API library reference (based on .NET Framework Version 4.5)

The ASP.NET Web API comprises the following namespaces:

Namespace	Purpose
`System.Net.Http`	This namespace comprises classes of HTTP attributes. This namespace provides extension methods for the `HttpRequestMessage` class.
`System.Net.Http.Formatting`	This comprises classes that can be used for serializing and deserializing the HTTP message body.
`System.Net.Http.Handlers`	This contains a collection of event handlers.
`System.Net.Http.Headers`	This namespace comprises classes that are related to `HttpHeaders`.
`System.Web.Http`	This namespace comprises classes of HTTP attributes. This namespace contains extension methods for the `HttpConfiguration` class.

Namespace	Purpose
`System.Web.Http.Controllers`	This namespace comprises a collection of classes that can control how the service would work on top of the HTTP protocol.
`System.Web.Http.Dependencies`	This namespace comprises a collection of classes that have a collection of dependency properties.
`System.Web.Http.Description`	This namespace comprises a collection of classes for web API description.
`System.Web.Http.Dispatcher`	This namespace comprises a collection of classes that are related to action dispatching.
`System.Web.Http.Filters`	This namespace comprises a collection of classes that are related to action-filter attributes.
`System.Web.Http.Hosting`	This namespace comprises a collection of classes that are used in HTTP hosting.
`System.Web.Http.Metadata`	This namespace comprises a collection of classes that are related to common metadata for data model.
`System.Web.Http.Metadata.Providers`	This namespace comprises a collection of classes that are related to metadata providers.
`System.Web.Http.ModelBinding`	This namespace comprises a collection of classes that are related to model binding.
`System.Web.Http.ModelBinding.Binders`	This namespace comprises a collection of classes of model binders.
`System.Web.Http.Routing`	This namespace comprises a collection of one or more classes that specifies the route properties.
`System.Web.Http.SelfHost`	This namespace comprises a collection of one or more classes that are related to HTTP self-hosted service.
`System.Web.Http.SelfHost.Channels`	This namespace comprises a collection of one or more classes that are related to classes for HTTP binding and security.
`System.Web.Http.Services`	This namespace comprises a collection of one or more classes that are related to default services.
`System.Web.Http.Tracing`	This namespace comprises a collection of one or more classes that are related to tracing.
`System.Web.Http.Validation`	This namespace comprises a collection of one or more classes that are related to model validation.
`System.Web.Http.Validation.Providers`	This namespace comprises a collection of one or more provider and factory classes that are related to model validation.
`System.Web.Http.Validation.Validators`	This namespace comprises a collection of one or more classes that are related to model validation.

Namespace	Purpose
System.Web.Http.ValueProviders	This namespace comprises a collection of one or more classes that are related to value providers.
System.Web.Http.ValueProviders.Providers	This namespace comprises a collection of one or more classes that are related to provider abstractions.
System.Web.Http.WebHost	This namespace comprises a collection of one or more classes that are related to web hosting.

References

The following are the reference sites:

- http://www.asp.net/web-api
- http://www.asp.net/web-api/overview/getting-started-with-aspnet-web-api/tutorial-your-first-web-api
- http://msdn.microsoft.com/en-us/library/hh833994%28v=vs.108%29.aspx

Index

Symbols

A

B

F

G

H

I

J

S

T

U

V

W

X

Y

About Packt Publishing

Packt, pronounced 'packed', published its first book "Mastering phpMyAdmin for Effective MySQL Management" in April 2004 and subsequently continued to specialize in publishing highly focused books on specific technologies and solutions.

Our books and publications share the experiences of your fellow IT professionals in adapting and customizing today's systems, applications, and frameworks. Our solution based books give you the knowledge and power to customize the software and technologies you're using to get the job done. Packt books are more specific and less general than the IT books you have seen in the past. Our unique business model allows us to bring you more focused information, giving you more of what you need to know, and less of what you don't.

Packt is a modern, yet unique publishing company, which focuses on producing quality, cutting-edge books for communities of developers, administrators, and newbies alike. For more information, please visit our website: `www.packtpub.com`.

About Packt Enterprise

In 2010, Packt launched two new brands, Packt Enterprise and Packt Open Source, in order to continue its focus on specialization. This book is part of the Packt Enterprise brand, home to books published on enterprise software – software created by major vendors, including (but not limited to) IBM, Microsoft and Oracle, often for use in other corporations. Its titles will offer information relevant to a range of users of this software, including administrators, developers, architects, and end users.

Writing for Packt

We welcome all inquiries from people who are interested in authoring. Book proposals should be sent to author@packtpub.com. If your book idea is still at an early stage and you would like to discuss it first before writing a formal book proposal, contact us; one of our commissioning editors will get in touch with you.

We're not just looking for published authors; if you have strong technical skills but no writing experience, our experienced editors can help you develop a writing career, or simply get some additional reward for your expertise.

[PACKT] enterprise
professional expertise distilled
PUBLISHING

Visual Studio 2012 and .NET 4.5 Expert Development Cookbook

ISBN: 978-1-84968-670-9 Paperback: 380 pages

Over 40 recipes for successfully mixing the powerful capabilities of .NET 4.5 and Visual Studio 2012

1. Step-by-step instructions to learn the power of .NET development with Visual Studio 2012
2. Filled with examples that clearly illustrate how to integrate with the technologies and frameworks of your choice
3. Each sample demonstrates key conceptsto build your knowledge of the architecture in a practical and incremental way

---

.Net Framework 4.5 Expert Programming Cookbook

ISBN: 978-1-84968-742-3 Paperback: 276 pages

Over 50 engaging recipes for learning advanced concepts of .NET Framework 4.5

1. Explores the advanced features of core .Net concepts in step-by-step detail
2. Understand great ways to enhance your website by securing against cross-site scripting attacks, enabling third party authentications, and embedding maps
3. Covers interesting real world projects with ASP.net, Silverlight, ADO.net, and Entity Framework

Please check **www.PacktPub.com** for information on our titles

[PACKT] enterprise
professional expertise distilled
PUBLISHING

Microsoft .NET Framework 4.5 Quickstart Cookbook

ISBN: 978-1-84968-698-3 Paperback: 226 pages

Get up to date with the exciting new features in .NET 4.5 Framework with these simple but incredibly effective recipes

1. Designed for the fastest jump into .NET 4.5, with a clearly designed roadmap of progressive chapters and detailed examples
2. A great and efficient way to get into .NET 4.5 and not only understand its features but clearly know how to use them, when, how and why
3. Covers Windows 8 XAML development, .NET Core (with Async/Await & reflection improvements), EF Code First & Migrations, ASP.NET, WF, and WPF

.NET 4.5 Parallel Extensions Cookbook

ISBN: 978-1-84969-022-5 Paperback: 336 pages

80 recipes to create scalable, task-based parallel programs using .NET 4.5

1. Create multithreaded applications using .NET Framework 4.5
2. Get introduced to .NET 4.5 parallel extensions and familiarized with .NET parallel loops
3. Use new data structures introduced by .NET Framework 4.5 to simplify complex synchronisation problems
4. Practical recipes on everything you will need to create task-based parallel programs

Please check **www.PacktPub.com** for information on our titles

Printed in Dunstable, United Kingdom

91371571R00127